PLAYS

OF THE

WILD WEST

Volume II
Grades 4–6

Published by Smith and Kraus, Inc.
PO Box 127, Lyme, NH 03768

Manufactured in the United States of America
First Edition: May 1997
10 9 8 7 6 5 4 3 2 1
Cover and Text Design by Julia Hill/Freedom Hill Design
Cover Illustration by Aline Ordman

The Library of Congress Cataloging-In-Publication Data
McCullough, L.E.

    Plays of the Wild West: grades4–6 / L.E. McCullough. —1st ed.
    p. cm. — (Young actors series)
    Includes bibliographical references.

    Summary: A collection of twelve original plays dramatizing songs, folklore, historical events, and larger-than-life characters of the Wild West.

    ISBN 1-57525-104-3
    1. Frontier and pioneer life—West (U.S.) —Juvenile drama.
    2. Children's plays, American. [1. Frontier and pioneer life—West (U.S.) —Drama. 2. West (U.S.) —Drama. 3. Plays.]
    I. Title. II. Series: Young Actors Series.

    PS3563.C35297P59   1997
    812'.54—dc21   97-14729
              CIP
                  AC

PLAYS OF THE WILD WEST

Volume II
Grades 4–6

L.E. McCullough

(p)04

YOUNG ACTORS SERIES

SK

A Smith and Kraus book

DEDICATION

To all our courageous ancestors—native peoples and settlers—who took part in one of the most tumultuous periods in human history, the Wild West. May we cherish and preserve the nation they created and the bountiful land they left us.

ACKNOWLEDGMENTS

The author wishes to thank the following for professional literary development and career support:

J.D. Nelson of Deadwood, South Dakota, a consummate actor and real-life cowboy; Joe Englander of Austin, Texas, whose photographs capture the ancient spirit of the modern West; Professor Dwayne Thorpe of Washington & Jefferson University, from whom I first heard many classic Western songs of his Kansas boyhood including *Zebra Dun*; folklorist W.K. McNeil, Ph.D. of the Ozark Folk Center, Mountain View, Arkansas; Lincoln Maazel of Pittsburgh; Jim Williams of Albuquerque, New Mexico; Linda Warder and her 5th-Grade Drama Club of Orchard Park Elementary School, Carmel, Indiana; Jana Foster of the Spanish Department, Indiana University-Purdue University at Indianapolis; my parents, who instilled my lifelong love of history with a Davy Crockett coonskin cap and Flint McCullough Wagon Train holster — *and* — my wife, Jane McCullough, a genuine Wild West pepperpot if there ever was one.

CONTENTS

FOREWORD

Backward, turn backward, oh time with your wheels,
Airplanes and wagons and automobiles;
Give me once more my sombrero and flaps,
Spurs, flannel shirt, slicker and chaps.
Put a six-shooter or two in my hand,
Show me a yearling to rope and to brand,
Out where the sagebrush is dusty and gray
Make me a cowboy again for a day.

— "Cowboy Again for a Day," Western folk song

The twelve plays in this book celebrate an epic period in American history — the transformation of the Western frontier from an unmapped wilderness inhabited by a few hundred thousand native tribespeople at the start of the 19th century into a fenced-off, dammed-up, staked-out region teeming with farms, factories, lumber mills, oil rigs, railroads, ranches and cities supporting millions of newcomers from around the world at the start of 20th. They cover a wide spectrum of historic events, ranging from the Battle of Wounded Knee and death of Sitting Bull to the slaughter of the American buffalo and the travels of the first mountain men. Most importantly for educators, *Plays of the Wild West* present not only well-known Western icons such as Jesse James, Geronimo, Wild Bill Hickok and Calamity Jane; they provide concise glimpses of the folks who did the real work of taming the frontier: homesteaders, railroaders, miners, missionaries, working cowboys and the West's first settlers, the Native Americans.

The story of the American West is, in fact, a diffuse rainbow of many remarkable stories celebrating the many remarkable people who left the familiar Old World for a New World of unceasing danger and unlimited promise. My ancestors first arrived on the North American continent from Wales in 1630 and settled in rural New England, each successive generation edging farther west until 1846 when they reached Wisconsin and Iowa, then the western boundary of the "civilized" United States. In 1865–66, my great-grandfather George McCollough served as a 19-year-old army corporal at Ft. Rice in Dakota Territory ("on the Indian Frontier," noted his obituary), and then returned home to St. Ansgar, Iowa, and an uneventful life as a teacher and commercial traveler. That was as far west as any of my family ventured until I taught at a folk music camp in Humboldt County, California, in the mid-1980s. Not much of a rousing pioneer pedigree, admittedly, yet I distinctly remember that the first toy I begged my parents to buy me as a child was a six-gun cap pistol like Hopalong Cassidy and The Lone Ranger carried. Even for modern Americans living far from the coyote's howl, the West exerts a continuing fascination.

The *Plays of the Wild West* series has been designed to combine with studies in other disciplines: history, costume, language, dance, music, social studies, etc. If you are a music teacher and want to add some more period songs and music to any of the plays, go ahead and make it a class project. *The Buffalo Hunters* can supplement lesson plans in environmental awareness and species preservation. If your class is doing *El Corrido de Gregorio Cortez* in conjunction with an area study of the southwestern United States, feel free to have the characters speak a few additional lines of Spanish and decorate the set with southwestern architecture and plants. Each play has enough real-life historical and cultural references to support a host of pre- or post-play activities that integrate easily with related curriculum areas.

Besides those children enrolled in the onstage cast, others can be included in the production as lighting and sound technicians, prop masters, script coaches and stage managers. *Plays of the Wild West* is an excellent vehicle for getting other members of the school and community involved in your project. Maybe there is a

Native American dance troupe or an accomplished performer of cowboy songs in your area; ask them to give a special concert/lecture when you present the play. Perhaps someone at your local historical society or library can give a talk about the frontier Army for *Ninth Cavalry to the Rescue!*; a theatre professor at a nearby college could add details about 19th-century popular entertainment for *Greasepaint and Ginthons: The Medicine Show Comes to Town*; is there someone at the art museum knowledgeable about Frederic Remington and other Western illustrators? Try utilizing the talents of local school or youth orchestra members to play incidental music...get the school art club to paint scrims and backdrops...see if a senior citizens' group might volunteer time to sew costumes...inquire whether a pioneer re-enactor club might bring samples of chuck wagon cuisine for *Vinegar Pete's Calico Whisker Pie*.

Most of all, have lots of fun. Realizing that many performing groups may have limited technical and space resources, I have kept sets, costumes and props minimal. However, if you do have the ability to build a Paiute wickiup for *Chief Sarah, The Indian Joan of Arc* or fashion a facsimile of Lawrence, Kansas, for *Jesse James: Blood on the Saddle* — go for it! Adding more music and dance and visual arts and crafts into the production involves more children and makes your play a genuinely multi-media event.

Similarly, I have supplied only basic stage and lighting directions. Blocking is really the province of the director; once you get the play up and moving, feel free to suit cast and action to your available population and experience level of actors. When figuring out how to stage these plays, I suggest you follow the venerable UYI Method — Use Your Imagination. If the play calls for a boat, bring in a wood frame, an old bathtub or have children draw a boat and hang as a scrim behind where the actors perform. Keep in mind the spirit of the old Andy Hardy musicals: "C'mon, everybody! Let's make a show!"

Age and gender. Obviously, your purpose in putting on the play is to entertain as well as educate; even though in the historical reality of 1879 a Texas Ranger company would have been all male, there is no reason these roles can't be played in *your* production by females. After all, the essence of the theatrical experience is to suspend us in time and ask us to believe that anything may be possible. Once again, UYI! Adult characters, such as grandparents or "old mountain men" or "bearded fiddlers," can be played by children costumed or made up to fit the part as closely as possible, or they can actually be played by adults. While *Plays of the Wild West* are intended to be performed chiefly by children, moderate adult involvement will add validation and let children know this isn't just a "kid project." If you want to get very highly choreographed or musically intensive, you will probably find a strategically placed onstage adult or two very helpful in keeping things moving smoothly. Still, *never* underestimate the capacity for even the youngest children to amaze you with their skill and ingenuity in making a show blossom.

Integrating authentic ethnic or period music is a great way to enhance your production. If you have questions about where to find recordings or written music of the tunes or genres included in these plays, or want some tips on performing and arranging them, I would be happy to assist you and may be reached by calling Smith & Kraus, Inc. at their toll-free customer service number, 1-800-895-4331.

Plays of the Wild West offers the opportunity to learn a little bit more about all of us who make up this amazing nation called the United States of America. So, shine up your spurs, give your lassos a twirl and get ready for some double-barreled, two-fisted, bronc-bustin' action. Happy trails!

L.E. McCullough, Ph.D.
Humanities Theatre Group
Indiana University-Purdue University at Indianapolis
Indianapolis, Indiana

PLAYS

WILD
WEST

Grades 4–6

THE BUFFALO HUNTERS

The buffalo is the largest wild animal native to North America, typically growing to a size of 12 feet in length, 6 feet in width and 2,000-3,000 pounds in weight. It has come to symbolize the rugged character of the American land and people. When the first Europeans came to the continent, there were over 125 million buffalo ranging freely across North America. Yet by 1889, only slightly more than 1,000 buffalo were left in the United States; they had been slaughtered by hunters for sport and by the Army in an effort to deprive the last rebellious Native American tribes of their main source of food. Early conservationists recognized the importance of preserving the buffalo. In 1872, President Grant signed the Yellowstone Park Act, which established the system of national parks, and a small herd of buffalo was taken to live in Yellowstone Park to be protected from hunters. According to the National Bison Association, there are now about 200,000 buffalo in the United States, most maintained in private herds. *The Rime of the Ancient Mariner,* from which Meredith Crombley Fitch-Wilkerson III quotes, is an epic poem by the English poet Samuel Taylor Coleridge (1772-1834); it describes the dire consequences to man of pointlessly killing animal life.

TIME: 1918; 1860s and '70s

PLACE: Cincinnati Zoo; The Great Plains

RUNNING TIME: 30 minutes

CAST: 31 actors, min. 15 boys, 3 girls

Wesley Martin, Age 71	Wesley Martin, Age 18-24
Benny Baxter	Bonnie Baxter
Johnny Reb	Billy Yank
Railroad Sutler	Pawnee Medicine Man
Buffalo Woman	Wolf

Antelope	Rabbit
4 Buffalo	2 Early People
California Joe	Wild Bill Hickok
Meredith Crombley Fitch-Wilkerson III	
Calamity Jane	Grand Duke Alexis
Grand Duke's Valet	Grand Duke's Armorer
Cheyenne Chief	Kiowa Chief
Comanche Chief	Arapaho Chief
Sitting Bull	2 Sioux Indians

STAGE SET: buffalo in cage at down right, sign on cage reading "Bison americanus"; 2 stools at down left

PROPS: cane, nickel, newspaper, list, pencil, blanket, 2 rifles, 2 stools, table, 4 tomahawks, 2 rattles

EFFECTS: Sounds — buffalo herd rumble; rifle shots

MUSIC: *Buffalo Gals, Buffalo Hunters*

COSTUMES: the elderly Wesley Martin and Benny and Bonnie Baxter dress in 1918 garb, with Martin wearing a long beard and a cane; young Wesley Martin, Fitch and California Joe wear buffalo hunter attire — plain white or dark woolen shirts, corduroy or denim breeches, high Western boots, wide-brimmed Western hats and bandanas; Calamity Jane dresses similarly to buffalo hunters but wears a fringed buckskin jacket; Wild Bill Hickok dresses a bit fancier with a red waist sash and a stylish frock coat and vest and a white shirt with cravat; Railroad Sutler wears storekeeper garb; Billy Yank dresses similar to buffalo hunters but has a blue jacket or Union Army hat; Johnny Reb dresses similar to buffalo hunters but has a grey jacket or Confederate Army hat; Buffalo Woman, Sitting Bull and other Native Americans dress with basic buckskin and one-piece, one-color smocks and moccasins embellished by feathers, blankets, headbands, beads, war paint on face; Buffalo and animal characters wear appropriate masks and body covering; Grand Duke Alexis wears a military-style outfit with lots of braiding and medals and a tall hat with plumage; Grand Duke's Armorer and Valet dress in servant livery

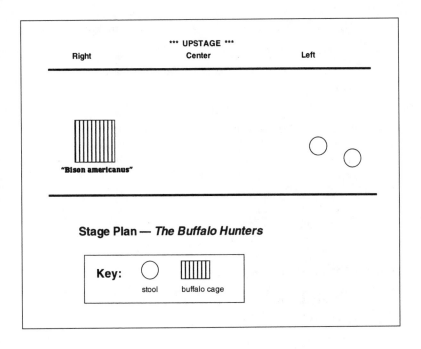

Right   Center   Left

"Bison americanus"

Stage Plan — *The Buffalo Hunters*

Key: ◯   ▥
         stool   buffalo cage

(LIGHTS UP RIGHT on BENNY BAXTER and BONNIE BAXTER standing at down right on either side of a buffalo cage at the Cincinnati Zoo.)

BENNY BAXTER: Gosh, sis, what kind of animal is that?

BONNIE BAXTER: I don't know, Benny. It sure is funny-looking! I've never seen anything like it!

BENNY BAXTER: Neither have I! Not in Cincinnati, anyway! Look how big it is! It must weigh two thousand pounds!

BONNIE BAXTER: Those horns look really sharp! How does it carry all that weight on those little hooves?

BENNY BAXTER: It's like a cow with shaggy fur all over it!

BONNIE BAXTER: Or a camel! See its hump?

BENNY BAXTER: I bet it could push over dad's Duesenberg! Maybe even a train!

(WESLEY MARTIN, an elderly man, enters from right, walking slowly with the aid of a cane toward center stage.)

BONNIE BAXTER: Let's ask that man. Maybe he knows what it's called.

BENNY BAXTER: Say, mister! Do you know what kind of animal this is?

(The man pauses, turns back to the children and studies the animal.)

WESLEY MARTIN: Let's see now…it *is* a curious beast. Why, the name is right here on the sign: "Bison americanus."

BONNIE BAXTER: *(shrugs)* What kind of language is that? Spanish? Maybe General Pershing brought it back from Europe!

WESLEY MARTIN: *(chuckles, points to the sign with his cane)* This is Latin, young lady. "Bison" means "wild ox." And "americanus"—

BONNIE BAXTER: Means "American"! This is an American wild ox?

WESLEY MARTIN; Better known to most folks as the "buffalo."

(Bonnie and Benny frown and shrug, perplexed.)

WESLEY MARTIN: You mean you kids never heard of a buffalo?

(Bonnie and Benny shake heads "no.")

WESLEY MARTIN: *(takes a nickel from his pocket and shows them)* Well, *that* animal is pictured on *this* nickel — and every other nickel like it in the United States of America since 1913!

BENNY BAXTER: *(points to cage)* So *that's* how the buffalo nickel got its name! Jeepers, mister, I never knew the buffalo was a real animal!

BONNIE BAXTER: We thought a buffalo was a mythical beast that lived in the olden times — you know, when our grandparents were young.

WESLEY MARTIN: That would have been when *I* was a boy. And I'm not *that* olden! But you youngsters are right; the American bison has all but vanished from our land. And, sad to say, it's men like me who drove him into the dust.

(LIGHTS OUT RIGHT; MUSIC: "Buffalo Gals" played offstage one time through on fiddle or banjo; LIGHTS UP LEFT on YOUNG WESLEY MARTIN sitting on stool at down left, reading a newspaper.)

WESLEY MARTIN (o.s.): The year was 1867, two years after the Civil War had ended. I'd grown up in Maryland, which didn't take sides during the war, and I figured I'd missed out on some mighty powerful adventure. Soon as I was eighteen I left home and headed West, where I found myself sitting in front of a railroad sutler's office in Fort Hays, Kansas, killing time and waiting for adventure to call my name.

(RAILROAD SUTLER enters from left holding a list and calls out to audience.)

RAILROAD SUTLER: Martin! Wesley Martin!

YOUNG WESLEY MARTIN: *(jumps up)* Right here, sir!

RAILROAD SUTLER: You don't have to burst my eardrums, son! *(checks off Wesley's name on list)* Sit down and wait till I call you again. *(exits left)*

(Young Wesley sits, impatiently; JOHNNY REB and BILLY YANK enter from left, stand on either side of Young Wesley and face audience; after a few moments, Johnny Reb addresses Young Wesley.)

JOHNNY REB: Are you-all finished perusing that periodical?

YOUNG WESLEY MARTIN: Beg pardon? Oh, the newspaper. Be my guest. *(hands Johnny Reb the newspaper)*

JOHNNY REB: Much obliged. You Yankees act like you've never heard the English language before.

BILLY YANK: You Rebels act like you've forgotten how to speak it.

(Johnny Reb and Billy Yank glower and bristle at each other; Young Wesley stands between them.)

YOUNG WESLEY MARTIN: I thought the war was over, gentlemen.

(Johnny Reb and Billy Yank back down.)

BILLY YANK: Fat lot of good winning did us Yanks. I went back home to Albany, and there wasn't a job in town.

JOHNNY REB: I returned to Mississippi, and there wasn't even a town. There must be thousands of us weary war veterans out here in the West — tens of thousands perhaps — seeking any sort of suitable employment to keep body and soul together in these starvation times.

(RAILROAD SUTLER enters from left holding a list and calls out to audience.)

RAILROAD SUTLER: Fitch Wilkerson Ill! Fitch Wilkerson Ill!

(MEREDITH CROMBLEY FITCH-WILKERSON III enters from left and taps the Railroad Sutler on shoulder.)

FITCH-WILKERSON: Hallo! Hallo, my good man!

RAILROAD SUTLER: Fitch Wilkerson Ill! *(checks off list)* What kind of picayune moniker is that?

FITCH-WILKERSON: Well, you see, my good man, you don't have the name quite correct. It's not Fitch-Wilkerson Ill. It's Fitch-Wilkerson Roman Numeral Three — the Third! My full name is Meredith Crombley Fitch-Wilkerson the Third. It's English, you know.

RAILROAD SUTLER: I *don't* know! And, it's still a darn picayune moniker! And I'm not your nor nobody else's good man! Now, stand over there with the rest of those yeggs!

(Young Wesley moves aside for Fitch-Wilkerson to stand between him and Billy Yank; Railroad Sutler moves to right of Johnny Reb and addresses the four young men.)

RAILROAD SUTLER: The Union Pacific Company is building a railroad from Nebraska to Utah. And the railroad workers need meat. Buffalo meat. Tons of it. Your job is to hunt it, skin it and bring it back here, so it can get cooked and the railroad can get built!

BILLY YANK: What do you want done with the critter's hide after we skin it?

RAILROAD SUTLER: You can make yourself a teepee for all I care. But there's tannery outfits in St. Louis and Chicago will pay one dollar eighty cents for the hide of a buffalo bull, three dollars and quarter for a cow, a dollar for a calf. Next question.

FITCH-WILKERSON: *(raises hand)* Sir! I say, my good man!

RAILROAD SUTLER: No more questions. Remember this: buffalo aren't as dumb as they look. There's seventy-five million of them, and they've been roaming this country for a thousand years, from the Potomac to the Pacific. They're fast and strong and can run all day without losing their wind. And, don't forget: a buffalo can smell a man a mile away. So you boys all better take regular baths. *(laughs)* Haw-haw-haw! *(exits left, followed by Johnny Reb and Billy Yank)*

FITCH-WILKERSON: *(to audience)* "God save thee, ancient Mariner, from the fiends that plague thee thus!"

YOUNG WESLEY MARTIN: Say, what are you wagging about, Fitch?

FITCH-WILKERSON: Oh, just a bit of poetry. "The Rime of the Ancient Mariner" by Coleridge. We studied it at Oxford.

YOUNG WESLEY MARTIN: Well, I haven't had much schooling myself, but I always admired a fellow who could versify. What's this here Rime about?

FITCH-WILKERSON: It tells the story of a sailor who shot a noble bird...and in doing so, brought bad luck upon his ship.

YOUNG WESLEY MARTIN: Sounds like some punkins! But I reckon we better leave off the poetry and pick up our supplies. Follow me, partner.

(YOUNG WESLEY and FITCH-WILKERSON exit left; LIGHTS OUT LEFT.)

WESLEY MARTIN *(o.s.)*: Well, Fitch and I struck out toward the buffalo range along the North Platte River that same day. We got to be good friends, soon as I could make out what he was saying. He'd left his home in England for the same reason I'd left mine — adventure! But that was in shorter supply than bloomers on a grizzly bear. For the first two weeks we didn't see any buffalo. Or any people. Until one day we came across a strange sight smack in the middle of the prairie.

(LIGHTS FADE UP CENTER and LEFT as Young Wesley and Fitch-Wilkerson, each carrying a rifle, enter from left and spy the PAWNEE MEDICINE MAN sitting at down center, his head sticking out of the blanket wrapped around him like a burial shroud.)

YOUNG WESLEY MARTIN: Look! It's a Pawnee medicine man.

FITCH-WILKERSON: Jolly good! Maybe he's seen something of a buffalo herd.

YOUNG WESLEY MARTIN: Hold on. They say old Indians go out to the prairie by themselves to die. Maybe we should let him be.

FITCH-WILKERSON: Well, if he's all *that* old, he's probably been here long enough to know where the buffalo are. My good sir, might we trouble you a moment? Have there been any buffalo in the neighborhood of late?

(Pawnee Medicine Man does not look at them and pauses a few moments before speaking. As he speaks, he addresses

audience and Young Wesley and Fitch-Wilkerson sit on either side of him.)

PAWNEE MEDICINE MAN: Once a long time ago, when the world was just beginning, all things lived in a deep, dark cave under the earth.

(BUFFALO WOMAN, WOLF, ANTELOPE, RABBIT, FOUR BUFFALO, TWO EARLY PEOPLE enter from left and right and assume frozen positions at mid center — standing, kneeling, lying down with heads bowed as if asleep.)

PAWNEE MEDICINE MAN: All the people were there, and all the animals. And great herds of buffalo. But everything was asleep. One day Buffalo Woman awoke.

(Buffalo Woman awakes and glides/dances among the other sleeping creatures, waking them with her touch.)

PAWNEE MEDICINE MAN: Buffalo Woman went among the other creatures and caused them to awake and come fully alive. She walked past Wolf...and Antelope...and Rabbit...and every living thing, preparing them for a great new world that lay above the ground.

(Buffalo Woman goes to down left and mimes pushing open a door above her head.)

PAWNEE MEDICINE MAN: Buffalo Woman went to a dark round place in the cave — and pushed it open! It was the sky of our world, and a great shining light poured into the cave through the hole.

(Buffalo Woman beckons to other creatures; they shrink back in fear.)

PAWNEE MEDICINE MAN: Buffalo Woman told the animals and the people to jump through the hole...but they were scared and would not go. Finally, a young buffalo rose up and bravely went through the hole into the world above.

(As Buffalo Woman mimes holding open the door, Buffalo #1 mimes jumping through a hole and exits left.)

PAWNEE MEDICINE MAN: Then a second buffalo went through... then a third and so on, until all the buffalo had gone out of the cave, with Wolf and Antelope and Rabbit and all the people and all the animals following behind, following the brave buffalo as they scattered over the prairie land, spreading everywhere in every direction through the sea of grass.

(Buffalo #1, 2 and 3, Wolf, Antelope, Rabbit and Two Early People jump through door held by Buffalo Woman and exit left; Buffalo Woman exits left last.)

PAWNEE MEDICINE MAN: And the people looked all around them and knew that this was their home...the home where they would live forever...together with the buffalo. *(lowers head)*

(YOUNG WESLEY AND FITCH-WILKERSON ARISE AND CIR-CLE BEHIND PAWNEE MEDICINE MAN, moving about the stage as if they are stalking buffalo.)

WESLEY MARTIN *(o.s.)*: Fitch and I both knew that story was more than just an old man's folktale. To the Indian of the Western Plains, the buffalo was the entire world. The buffalo provided food, clothing, shelter, weapons and fuel. Indians sang about the buffalo and made up dances to help hunt it. The buffalo was an important part of the Indians' religion, and they respected it as an equal being. To us hunters, though, the buffalo was just another hide for sale.

(SOUND FADES UP: rumble of approaching buffalo herd; Young Wesley and Fitch-Wilkerson are at mid center; Fitch-Wilkerson looks to stage left and grabs Young Wesley's arm.)

FITCH-WILKERSON: Listen! To the south!
YOUNG WESLEY MARTIN: It sounds like the mightiest roar of thunder ever rolled out of the heavens!
FITCH-WILKERSON: Look! Beyond the rise! Do you see them?
YOUNG WESLEY MARTIN: Why, it's a buffalo herd on the run! Great Jupiter, it must be five miles wide!
FITCH-WILKERSON: And fifteen or twenty long. Let's have a go!

(Young Wesley and Fitch-Wilkerson kneel and begin shooting, slowly and methodically; SOUND: rifle shots.)

WESLEY MARTIN *(o.s.)*: The barrels of our fifty-caliber Sharps rifles nearly melted from the heat of firing. We killed two hundred fifty buffalo in the first hour — beginner's luck, we reckoned — but the herd kept coming, a rich, brown river rolling along the green, grassy prairie, never stopping, never veering from its headlong stampede northward. Finally, the tail of the herd stopped, and lay down for a rest. We crept closer, a hundred feet away, and took up firing again.

FITCH-WILKERSON: *(shoots; SOUND: rifle shot)* Wesley, this is absolutely incredible! It's like shooting fish in a barrel! *(shoots; SOUND: rifle shot)*

YOUNG WESLEY MARTIN: I got it figured out, Fitch. You drop the lead cow. But make sure she doesn't die right off. Then her calves will come up to her, and you can get them as they watch her die. *(shoots; SOUND: rifle shot)*

WESLEY MARTIN *(o.s.)*: We kept on killing all night. Finally, I felt a little sick at the slaughter, the huge glassy eyes of the beasts staring up at us as they kicked out the last shreds of life in the bloody dust.

(Young Wesley and Fitch-Wilkerson stand over a dead buffalo.)

FITCH-WILKERSON: "And I had done a hellish thing, and it would work them woe. For all averred, I had killed the bird that made the breeze to blow."

(LIGHTS OUT LEFT AND CENTER.)

WESLEY MARTIN *(o.s.)*: Fitch had some strange ideas about poetry, but he could sure handle a rifle. From the fifteenth of September to the fifteenth of October, we each killed over two thousand buffalo. Now it was time to haul the meat and hides back to Fort Hays, about two hundred miles away. We passed through long stretches where other hunters had been before us — thousands of dead buffalo rotting on the ground, surrounded by hungry packs of wolves and coyotes eagerly attending to what the careless hunters had left behind, the sky filled with screaming buzzards circling overhead. Finally, we arrived back in civilization.

CALIFORNIA JOE *(o.s.)*: Eeeeee-haah!

(LIGHTS UP LEFT AND CENTER; MUSIC: "Buffalo Gals" played offstage one time through on fiddle or banjo; CALIFORNIA JOE sits on a stool behind a table at down left, slapping his knees in rhythm to the music as Young Wesley and Fitch-Wilkerson enter from left; MUSIC FADES OUT.)

CALIFORNIA JOE: Howdy, fellers! You look you just come in off the buffalo trail! Set yourselves down and name your poison!

(California Joe stands and offers stool to Fitch-Wilkerson, who sits; Young Wesley sits on the other stool.)

CALIFORNIA JOE: *(shakes hands with Fitch-Wilkerson and Young Wesley)* My name's Joe, California Joe. I'm an old-time mountain man and army scout, wild as a jaybird stallion and stubborn as a flop-eared mule. Just got back from scouting for Custer and the Seventh Cavalry along the Washita. Oh, he's mad as a March hare, that Custer! Say, there's Wild Bill Hickok and his lady friend, Calamity Jane!

(WILD BILL HICKOK and CALAMITY JANE enter from left, shake hands with California Joe.)

CALIFORNIA JOE: Say, Bill, these two young fellers have just come back from their first buffalo hunt. Wild Bill here's been hunting the buffalo since '65.

WILD BILL HICKOK: Buffalo hides are good as gold these days. Better even. Why, folks will pay just to watch you kill the darn things!

CALAMITY JANE: Last year Bill got hired by a bunch of rich Easterners to escort them on a buffalo hunt. There was a Senator from Massachusetts.

CALIFORNIA JOE: And a newspaper editor from New York City.

WILD BILL HICKOK: They were shooting buffalo from the train windows.

CALAMITY JANE: "Slaughter of the Millionaires" the papers called it.

CALIFORNIA JOE: And when Bill got to Red Willow, who was there but Buffalo Bill Cody and Grand Duke Alexis of Russia!

WILD BILL HICKOK: The son of the Russian Czar himself.

(GRAND DUKE ALEXIS enters from right and strides to center, followed by the GRAND DUKE'S VALET, who carries the Grand Duke's hunting jacket and hat, and the GRAND DUKE'S ARMORER, who carries the Grand Duke's rifle.)

CALAMITY JANE: Oh, it was quite a spectacle. That Grand Duke had more outfits than Lady Vanderbilt.

(Grand Duke's Valet puts on the Grand Duke's hunting jack-

et and hat; Grand Duke's Armorer hands rifle to the Grand Duke, who fumbles with it clumsily.)

CALIFORNIA JOE: Buffalo Bill was earning his greenbacks that day, I'll warrant. Why, the Grand Duke was a grand fluke! He couldn't hit the broad side of a buffalo with a steamboat!

(Grand Duke Alexis shoots wildly in the air as Valet and Armorer duck.)

CALAMITY JANE: Finally, Cody got so disgusted, he shot a buffalo—
CALIFORNIA JOE: And led the Grand Duke right up to it, so he stood not four feet away and said—
WILD BILL HICKOK: "Lexy, if you don't shoot that critter soon, I'm afraid it's gonna die of pure boredom!"

(Grand Duke Alexis aims at the ground and shoots. SOUND: rifle shot.)

GRAND DUKE'S VALET & GRAND DUKE'S ARMORER: Hip, hip, hurrah!
CALAMITY JANE, CALIFORNIA JOE & WILD BILL HICKOK: Hip, hip, hurrah!
VALET, ARMORER, CALAMITY JANE, CALIFORNIA JOE & WILD BILL HICKOK: Hip, hip, hurrah!

(Grand Duke Alexis, Grand Duke's Armorer, Grand Duke's Valet exit right; MUSIC: "The Buffalo Hunters.")

WILD BILL HICKOK: (SINGS)
Come all you pretty fair maids these lines to you I write
We're going on the range in which we take delight
We're going on the range as we poor hunters do
So those tenderfooted fellows can stay at home with you
CALAMITY JANE: (SINGS)
Our game it is the antelope, the buffalo, elk and deer
They roam the broad prairies without the least of fear
We rob them of their robes, in which we think no harm
To buy us chuck and clothing to keep our bodies warm
CALIFORNIA JOE: (SINGS)
It's all of the day long as we go tramping round
In search of the buffalo that we may shoot him down
Our guns upon our shoulders, our belts of forty rounds
We send them up Salt River to their happy hunting grounds

(LIGHTS FADE OUT CENTER AND LEFT.)

WESLEY MARTIN *(o.s.)*: Next spring, Fitch and I went out again on buffalo trail. We spent the next ten years following the big herds from Wyoming to Texas, and we met some mighty interesting characters along the way as they criss-crossed the growing West — Bat Masterson, Doc Holliday, Big Nose Kate Elder, the Earps. But with each passing year, the buffalo herds grew smaller and harder to find. Over four million were killed by hunters between 1872 and 1874 alone. And the Indian tribes who had depended for centuries upon the buffalo for their existence grew ever more angry and desperate.

(LIGHTS UP CENTER on FOUR INDIAN CHIEFS sitting on the ground in a semi-circle facing audience; each Chief holds a tomahawk in his lap.)

CHEYENNE CHIEF: My brothers, the White Father in Washington talks with forked tongue. He allows the Long Rifles to trespass on our lands and hunt buffalo; but *our* braves are forbidden to hunt, though our people starve.

KIOWA CHIEF: One of the bluecoat leaders, Colonel Dodge, tells his troopers: "Kill every buffalo you can. Every buffalo dead is an Indian gone."

COMMANCHE CHIEF: Our women cry through the night for their children who die each day, bellies empty because the reservation agents steal the food the treaty has promised us.

ARAPAHO CHIEF: If we do not fight back now, we will vanish from the earth like the buffalo. What say you, my brothers? Who will follow me on the war path to avenge the buffalo?

(Arapaho Chief places his tomahawk into the semi-circle, and the Four Chiefs extend their tomahawks to touch his: LIGHTS OUT CENTER.)

WESLEY MARTIN *(o.s.)*: The Indians were driven onto the war path — many times. But great warriors though they were, they could not defeat the bluecoats, and they could not bring back the buffalo. After decades of warfare, the Indian tribes gave up their fight and surrendered, moving onto reservations where they starved and suffered from disease. And by 1884, Fitch and I had hung up our rifles, too. Instead of hunting live buffalo, we earned our living picking up the acres of buffalo bones that lay across the prairie like a winter frost, shipping them back East in railroad cars to be ground up for crop fertilizer. Why, you could walk a thousand miles in any direction and never be out of sight of a dead buffalo — and never *in* sight of a *live* one. Yep — we were scavengers now, too, just like the wolves and buzzards.

(LIGHTS UP LEFT on SITTING BULL and TWO SIOUX INDIANS; Sitting Bull looks skyward toward audience, while the Two Sioux Indians dance on either side of him, shaking rattles.)

WESLEY MARTIN *(o.s.)*: But come 1890, the Sioux chief Sitting Bull began having dreams about the buffalo herds returning...and when they returned, the white man would vanish. Sitting Bull was a powerful dreamer and a great medicine man, and in December, the Plains Tribes gathered at Wounded Knee, South Dakota — under the watchful eye of the U.S. Army — to begin a Ghost Dance they were sure would bring back the buffalo.

(Indians dance for a few seconds, then rifle shots ring out. SOUND: rifle shots. Sitting Bull and Indians fall down, dead.)

FITCH-WILKERSON *(o.s.)*: "He prayeth best, who loveth best all things both great and small...For the dear God who loveth us, He made and loveth all."

(LIGHTS OUT LEFT; LIGHTS UP RIGHT on BENNY BAXTER, BONNIE BAXTER and grownup WESLEY MARTIN in front of buffalo cage.)

BENNY BAXTER: *(points to cage)* Gee willikers, mister! Is this the last buffalo left in America?

WESLEY MARTIN: Not quite. There is a small herd in Yellowstone National Park kept safe from hunters by the national park service. And in 1905 the American Bison Society was created by conservationists to educate folks about this precious part of our country's natural heritage.

BONNIE BAXTER: Well, at least we still have the buffalo on the nickel. And look, there's an Indian on the other side!

WESLEY MARTIN: I guess they rightly belong together, wouldn't you say?

BENNY BAXTER: Say, mister, are you sorry you killed all those buffalo when you were young?

WESLEY MARTIN: I am sad, son — very sad. But back then, we didn't know the damage we were doing. Your generation is smarter about the world, and it's up to you to make sure something like this never happens again.

BENNY BAXTER: To the buffalo.

BONNIE BAXTER: Or the Indian.

WESLEY MARTIN: *(looks toward audience)* You know, when I close my eyes, I can still see those big herds out on the prairie. *(closes eyes)* And sometimes, when the wind is just right, I can hear the old ballads we sang on the buffalo trail.

(MUSIC: "The Buffalo Hunters"; Entire Cast enters onstage.)

WESLEY MARTIN: *(SINGS)*
The buffalo is the largest and the noblest of the band
He sometimes refuses to throw us up his hand
With shaggy mane thrown forward and head raised to the sky
He seems to say, "We're coming, boys, so hunter, mind your eye!"

ENTIRE CAST: *(SINGS)*
Come all you pretty fair maids these lines to you I write
We're going on the range in which we take delight
We're going on the range as we poor hunters do
So those tenderfooted fellows can stay at home with you

(LIGHTS OUT; MUSIC: "Buffalo Gals" played offstage one time through on fiddle or banjo as cast exits.)

THE END

Buffalo Gals
(traditional, arranged by L.E. McCullough)

The Buffalo Hunters
(traditional, arranged by L.E. McCullough)

Come —— all you pret- ty fair maids these lines to you I

write; We're go- ing on the range —— in

which we take de- light; We're go- ing on the

range —— as we poor hun- ters do; So those

ten- der- foot- ed fel- lows can stay at home with you

CHIEF SARAH, THE INDIAN JOAN OF ARC

Sarah Winnemucca (1844-1891) was a member of the Paiute tribe of Nevada. She realized while very young that the only chance the Native Americans had to defend themselves against the encroachment of white settlers was to learn how to read, write and speak English — and then fight to persuade other Americans to help the Indian win justice. After serving as an Army scout and interpreter and helping save many of her tribe from harm by corrupt Indian agents, Sarah was elected a chief of the Paiutes. She made several trips to the East to lecture on the plight of the Indians and to campaign for fair treatment. She started schools for Indian children and wrote and published a book. Even the whites who fought against Chief Sarah admired her courage. They called her "The Indian Joan of Arc," after the brave young French young woman who led her nation to victory in the Middle Ages.

TIME: November, 1891

PLACE: A homestead in Montana

RUNNING TIME: 20 minutes

CAST: 21 actors, min. 10 boys, 14 girls

Elma Winnemucca, Adult	Sarah Winnemucca, Age 5
Elma Winnemucca, Age 11	Sarah Winnemucca, Age 16
Elma Winnemucca, Age 15	Sarah Winnemucca, Adult
Winter Blossom	Captain Truckee
Chief Winnemucca	Sarah's Mother
Sarah's Aunt	Sister Fidelia
3 Paiute War Chiefs	General Howard
Washington Post Reporter	Dr. Buchanan

Mrs. Olé Bull   Mary Mann
Elizabeth Peabody

STAGE SET: 2 stools at down left

PROPS: small drum, spear, letter, 2 school books, 2 stools, notebook, hard-bound book

MUSIC: *Paiute Spirit Song*

COSTUMES: Mary Mann, Mrs. Olé Bull, Elizabeth Peabody and Elma and Sarah Winemucca as adults dress as typical of American women of 1870s-'80s — dark ankle-length skirt and white blouse; Elma and Sarah as children wear Native American girl's dress of 1850s — one-piece buckskin tunics, moccasins, headbands; Sarah during her days as scout dresses in jeans, bucksin shirt, Stetson hat, boots; other characters dress according to occupation: Sister Fidelia as a Catholic nun, General Howard as a military officer, Dr. Buchanan as a professor, Captain Truckee and other Paiutes as mid-century Native Americans

(LIGHTS UP RIGHT. At down right a middle-aged Paiute woman, ELMA WINNEMUCCA, stands facing audience, beating a small drum in a slow, steady rhythm; she begins chanting and a child, WINTER BLOSSOM, enters from right and observes her.)

ELMA WINNEMUCCA:
All the white-cloud eagles—
Lift her with your wings.
Take her to Mother Eagle,
Home of all spirits.
Lift her with your wings.

(Elma Winnemucca turns and addresses Winter Blossom.)

ELMA WINNEMUCCA: Winter Blossom, my grandchild! Is this not a fine day to travel?

WINTER BLOSSOM: It is a fine day, grandmother. But who is going to travel? And where?

ELMA WINNEMUCCA: My sister, Chief Sarah Winnemucca. *(points skyward)* Her soul is traveling to meet Mother Eagle in the land of the spirits. That is why I chant the Paiute Spirit Song — to guide her way.

WINTER BLOSSOM: I am glad Chief Sarah is going to meet Mother Eagle. But I am sorry she has died. I wish I had known her better.

ELMA WINNEMUCCA: Chief Sarah was a remarkable woman. Did you know she wrote the first book published in English by an Indian? And started the first school taught and administered by Indians? She spoke five languages and was an Army scout and chief of her tribe.

WINTER BLOSSOM: *(sits on ground and motions for Elma Winnemucca to sit also)* Please tell me, grandmother, about Chief Sarah. Tell me everything she did.

(LIGHTS FADE OUT RIGHT; LIGHTS FADE UP LEFT and CENTER.)

ELMA WINNEMUCCA: Sarah was born in 1844 — forty-seven years ago — in the Nightingale Mountains of western Nevada. The Paiute people had lived there for centuries, in the shadow of beautiful Pyramid Lake, which they believed was a magic lake and home to many good spirits. The Paiutes were at peace with themselves and with the mountains and desert around them. But when Little Sarah was five years old, and I was but an infant, white men came into the Paiute country, seeking gold and bringing death.

(LITTLE SARAH enters from left holding a handful of bright desert flowers; she addresses audience.)

LITTLE SARAH: My name is Thocmetony — the Paiute word for shellflower. These flowers I make as an offering. I offer them to Mother Eagle and all great spirits. I offer them for strength and for wisdom. I offer them as thanks for the great love you show your people.

(Little Sarah lays flowers on ground; CHIEF WINNEMUCCA, SARAH'S MOTHER, SARAH'S AUNT and CAPTAIN TRUCKEE burst onstage from right and gather at down center; SARAH'S MOTHER AND SARAH'S AUNT are weeping; Chief Winnemucca, carrying a spear, addresses Captain Truckee.)

CHIEF WINNEMUCCA: I tell you, Captain Truckee, we must get revenge! Revenge for what the white man has done to our people!

CAPTAIN TRUCKEE: Chief Winnemucca, the white men *you* want to kill had *nothing* to do with the men who killed our people. You want to kill them only because they are white men. You want revenge, not justice!

SARAH'S MOTHER: White men killed my brother, who was fishing for his family's supper!

SARAH'S AUNT: White men burned our winter store of pine nuts to dig their gold mine! They want us to starve!

CAPTAIN TRUCKEE: Does not my own beloved son lie with your dead? More killing will not bring them back to life!

CHIEF WINNEMUCCA: *(points finger at Captain Truckee)* You are my father. You taught me to be strong and without fear. *(brandishes spear)* As chief of the Paiutes, I declare war upon the white man! Aiiiiiiee!

SARAH'S MOTHER & SARAH'S AUNT: Aiiiiiiee! Aiiiiiiee! Aiiiiiiee!

CAPTAIN TRUCKEE: Wait! *(points to Little Sarah)* Behold that child. If you make war, she and all our children will not live to see their first courtship.

LITTLE SARAH: Grandfather?

CAPTAIN TRUCKEE: What is it, Thocmetony?

LITTLE SARAH: Why do the white men want to kill our people?

CAPTAIN TRUCKEE: Come here, little one, and I will tell you a story.

LITTLE SARAH: Yes, Grandfather. *(goes to Captain Truckee)*

CAPTAIN TRUCKEE: *(kneels on one knee next to Little Sarah)* At the beginning of the world, there was a family that had four children. There was a dark girl and a dark boy, and a light girl and a light boy. At first, these children played well together. But one day, they began to quarrel.

SARAH'S MOTHER: "Why are you so cruel to each other?" asked their mother. "It is wrong to argue and fight."

SARAH'S AUNT: But the children continued to quarrel, until one day their father became angry.

CHIEF WINNEMUCCA: "Go away from each other, you wicked children! Go across the mighty ocean and do not speak to each other ever again!"

CAPTAIN TRUCKEE: So the dark girl and boy went away and grew into a large nation — the nation of Indians. And the light girl and boy went away and grew into the large nation of white people. And, says the legend, one day the whites will come across the ocean and visit the Indians and make peace between the nations.

LITTLE SARAH: But, grandfather, I do not want to meet the white men! With their white eyes and hairy faces, they look like owls!

CAPTAIN TRUCKEE: Do not be afraid, Thocmetony. We must learn the ways of our white brothers. *(rises, addresses others)* My people, the white men are already here in our land. We cannot drive them away. We must learn to live together — or the Great Spirit will turn us all into dust. *(takes a letter from his shirt pocket and holds it up)* Do you see this? This is my friend, my white-rag friend. It was given to me by the soldier John Frémont, who I guided to California in the Americans' war against Mexico. When I take it to the white man, it can ask for something to eat. It can ask for horses. It can ask for peace. *(hands it to Little Sarah)* You must learn to talk to the white man, Thocmetony. You must learn the language of the white-rag friend. It has great power.

(LIGHTS OUT; characters exit left.)

ELMA WINNEMUCCA (O.S.): Soon after, Captain Truckee took Sarah and me to the trading post at Genoa, Nevada, on the shores of Lake Tahoe. There we lived with a white family — Major William Ormsby and his wife, Margaret. The Ormsbys were very kind and taught us the ways of white people. How to dress like white people with skirts and shoes, how to eat like white people with forks and napkins. One day Sarah asked Mrs. Ormsby how to speak the language of Captain Truckee's white-rag friend — and Mrs. Ormsby showed Sarah how to read and write.

(LIGHTS UP LEFT on TEENAGE SARAH and YOUNG ELMA sitting on stools at down left, each eagerly reading a school book.)

ELMA WINNEMUCCA: *(o.s.)* In 1860, Sarah and I went to San Jose, California. There, a white friend of Captain Truckee's paid for us to attend a real school! It was a convent school for girls taught by the Sisters of Notre Dame, and it was the most wonderful place we had ever seen.

TEENAGE SARAH: Grammar, history, geography, arithmetic and music! Elma, I want to know every subject in the world!

YOUNG ELMA: Yesterday, Sister Ramona taught us needlework. I made a saddle blanket for father's horse.

TEENAGE SARAH: How I love reading! I hope we shall stay here forever!

(SISTER FIDELIA enters from left.)

TEENAGE SARAH & YOUNG ELMA: Good morning, Sister Fidelia!

SISTER FIDELIA: Children, I have sad news. You must leave the school at once.

TEENAGE SARAH: But, Sister, how can this be? We have only been here three weeks!

SISTER FIDELIA: I am very sorry. But some of the parents of the white children do not think Indian children should be educated. They have threatened to remove their children from the school. Without their money, the school cannot stay open. *(exits left)*

YOUNG ELMA: Sarah, I do not understand white people. They say we must become like them. And when we try to learn, they tell us we cannot.

TEENAGE SARAH: White people have many secrets. Perhaps the answers are in these books. I will continue to study them, even if I cannot attend the white man's school.

(LIGHTS OUT LEFT; Sarah and Elma exit left.)

ELMA WINNEMUCCA: *(o.s.)* When my sister and I returned to our people in Nevada, many terrible things had taken place. White men had discovered silver in the Pine Nut Mountains. In their mad hunger for riches, they destroyed the woods and meadows that gave the Paiutes our food. They drove away game and threw garbage into the streams. They made us live on reservations and allowed corrupt agents to steal our food. Finally, the Paiutes could stand no more, and the chiefs called a council of war.

(LIGHTS UP CENTER on THREE PAIUTE WAR CHIEFS and SARAH WINNEMUCCA AS ADULT gathered in semi-circle facing audience.)

WAR CHIEF #1: The white man has gone too far this time. If we do not fight, every Indian will die!

SARAH WINNEMUCCA: *(shows letter)* I have written a letter to Major Douglass telling how the Indian has been cheated. He has sent it to Washington to President Johnson, chief of all the whites.

WAR CHIEF #2: Bah! The white men are like coyotes. Always barking, always stealing. They make heap of talk. And their talk is no good.

WAR CHIEF #3: We have only two choices: to do nothing and starve to death, or steal cattle and be shot by soldiers. *(stands)* Who will die a warrior with me?

SARAH WINNEMUCCA: *(stands)* No! The white men are like the stars over our heads. Can you reach up and blot out those stars? The sky will be filled with even more! *(waves letter)* Put your weapons aside...let our white-rag friend talk to the President.

(ELMA WINNEMUCCA AS TEEN dashes in, breathless, from left and collapses on ground.)

SARAH WINNEMUCCA: Elma!

TEENAGE ELMA WINNEMUCCA: Soldiers came to our village at Muddy Lake...the young men were away, hunting...for no reason, the soldiers opened fire on women and children and old men, all of them killed, village set on fire...I saw soldiers take babies and small children and throw them into the fires, and laugh while they burned alive...Sarah, our mother and our baby brother are dead! *(falls unconscious)*

(War Chief #1 stands, grabs letter from Sarah.)

WAR CHIEF #1: This is what comes of talk! *(crumples letter)* White man's words mean nothing!

(Three War Chiefs exit left, helping Teenage Elma offstage as Sarah stands down center and broods, head lowered.)

ELMA WINNEMUCCA *(o.s.)*: And so began ten months of bloody war, which the Paiutes lost. Our family was broken apart. I went to live in Montana. Our father and most of the tribe were sent to a reservation in Oregon. But Sarah stayed in our homeland to fight for the Indian cause. She worked for the Army as a scout and an interpreter. She wrote letters to newspapers telling how white agents cheated the Indians. And after fighting in battle to lead her people to safety during the Bannock War of 1878, she was chosen as tribal chief — the first time a woman had ever been thus honored by the Paiutes. A few months later at Fort Vancouver, she spoke with General Howard, an important Army leader.

(GENERAL HOWARD enters from right and crosses to center where he sharply salutes Sarah, who returns salute.)

SARAH WINNEMUCCA: General Howard, you have always treated the Indian with fairness. Why can you not help us fight corrupt agents?

GENERAL HOWARD: Sarah, under the white man's system of government, warriors don't make laws. The Army only carries out the orders of its citizens.

SARAH WINNEMUCCA: But *I* am a citizen.

GENERAL HOWARD: That is true. And as a citizen, you have the right to speak out against what you see are wrongs. Why don't you go to the American people and tell them what conditions are like on the reservations? I will give you a letter of introduction and recommendation. *(exits right)*

SARAH WINNEMUCCA: Thank you, General. *(salutes, then faces audience in SPOTLIGHT at center)* Ladies and gentlemen of of San Francisco, my name is Sarah Winnemucca, chief of the Paiute tribe. I speak to you today concerning the great harm done to the native people of our land — the American Indian. When your red brothers and sisters are harmed by lies and treachery, you are harmed also. If you will help me, I promise to educate my people and make them law-abiding citizens of the United States. With your help, I will go to Washington and speak to the President. I will expose all the rascals. My mouth will not be sealed. *(curtseys, exits right)*

(LIGHTS UP LEFT as REPORTER with notebook enters from left and stands at down left, facing audience.)

REPORTER: Sarah Winnemucca went to Washington, D.C. in the spring of 1880. I covered the story for the *Washington Post*, and I never met anyone as impressive as that little Indian maid from Nevada. She was as well-spoken and well-informed as any college professor — why, she speaks five languages! Of course, the Bureau of Indian Affairs didn't want her to lecture, and they tried to muzzle her pretty hard. But she stuck to her guns, all the while behaving like a lady — more so, in fact, than most of the Washington society matrons I've come across. She even got to meet President Hayes, and he ordered the head of Indian Affairs to give Sarah's tribe land, food and housing. But when she returned to the West, the reservation agents refused to follow the orders — and the Indians starved and suffered through the long cold winter. *(holds up notebook)* Sarah's "white-rag friend" had betrayed her once again. *(exits left)*

ELMA WINNEMUCCA *(o.s.):* But Sarah did not give up. She returned to Fort Vancouver and taught at the Indian school. Three years later, she went back East, this time to Boston. She would no longer try to win over the minds of government bureaucrats...she would set about winning the hearts of the nation.

(LIGHTS UP CENTER as, ELIZABETH PEABODY, MARY MANN and MRS. OLÉ BULL enter from left and stand at down center, perpendicular to audience and facing left; DR. BUCHANAN and SARAH, carrying a hard-bound book, enter from right and face them.)

DR. BUCHANAN: I am Dr. Buchanan of Boston University. We would like to thank Mrs. Olé Bull, the widow of the great Norwegian violinist, for hosting our speaker — the Indian Joan of Arc, Chief Sarah Winnemucca.

(Mrs. Olé Bull curtseys; Dr. Buchanan steps behind Sarah, who addresses the group.)

SARAH WINNEMUCCA: My journey has been long, but it has been

good. Thanks to the support of my friends Elizabeth Peabody and Mary Mann, I have spoken to thousands of people in scores of cities. I have gathered thousands of signatures for a petition that I presented to the Congress of the United States. And now, I have written and published a book: "Life Among the Paiutes, Their Wrongs and Claims."

(Elizabeth Peabody, Mary Mann, Mrs. Olé Bull and Dr. Buchanan applaud.)

SARAH WINNEMUCCA: I have been told that this is the first book published in English by any American Indian. I wish it could have been a happier book. Though our past and present are filled with sadness, I believe our future can be different. To this end, I am returning to the West, where I will start a school for Indians taught by Indians themselves. This school — instead of wiping out Indian culture — will preserve it.

(Elizabeth Peabody, Mary Mann, Mrs. Olé Bull and Dr. Buchanan applaud and cheer; Sarah exits left, followed by Mary Mann, Mrs. Olé Bull and Dr. Buchanan, still applauding.)

ELIZABETH PEABODY: Sarah started her school near Lovelock, Nevada, on 160 acres of land donated by Senator Leland Stanford of California, who had helped finance the Central Pacific Railroad and had long been interested in helping the Indian become educated. The school was very successful. A teacher from Wisconsin came to study Sarah's methods and found that her Indian pupils were superior in speaking, writing and drawing to the pupils who attending a nearby whites-only school. But Sarah was not able to enjoy her success. Though only in her early forties, her health was failing. She suffered from rheumatism and tuberculosis. After only two years, Sarah had to close her school. She died October 17, 1891, while visiting her sister Elma in Montana. *(exits left)*

(LIGHTS OUT LEFT; LIGHTS UP RIGHT on Elma Winnemucca and Winter Blossom, both seated on ground.)

WINTER BLOSSOM: My goodness, grandmother, that is a remarkable story!

ELMA WINNEMUCCA: Most remarkable is that Chief Sarah never gave up her struggle against bigotry and corruption...and the struggle for Indian children to learn the power of the "white-rag friend." I remember the last words she said...

(SPOTLIGHT LEFT ON SARAH WINNEMUCCA standing at down left.)

SARAH WINNEMUCCA: My Indian friends, a few years ago you owned this great country. Today the white man owns it all, and you own nothing. Do you know what did it? Education. You have brains same as the whites, and your children have brains. I entreat you to get hold of this school and give your support by sending your children, old and young, to it. And when they grow up to manhood and womanhood, they will bless you."

(SPOTLIGHT OUT; Elma Winnemucca begins beating a small drum in a slow, steady rhythm; she and WINTER BLOSSOM sing, facing audience. MUSIC: "Paiute Spirit Song.")

ELMA WINNEMUCCA & WINTER BLOSSOM: *(SING)*
All the white-cloud eagles—
Lift her with your wings.
Take her to Mother Eagle,
Home of all spirits.
Lift her with your wings.
As she lifted up her people,
Lift Chief Sarah with your wings.

(LIGHTS OUT.)

THE END

Paiute Spirit Song
(words & music by L.E. McCullough)

All the white-cloud ea- gles; lift her with your wings.

Take her to Mo- ther Ea- gle, home of all spi- rits.

Lift her with your wings. As she lif- ted up her

peo- ple, lift Chief Sa- rah with your wings.

EL CORRIDO DE GREGORIO CORTEZ
THE BALLAD OF GREGORIO CORTEZ

Some of the stirring episodes that took place along the Western frontier were immortalized in song and remain with us today. *El Corrido de Gregorio Cortez* is a folk ballad that has been sung along the Texas-Mexico border for nearly a hundred years and is based on a true incident. In South Texas in 1901, a Spanish-speaking farm worker was unjustly accused by an English-speaking sheriff of stealing a horse. Because neither the worker nor the sheriff could understand each other's language, confusion led to distrust and distrust led to fear; within seconds, pistols were produced and blood was shed, resulting in the ruin of many innocent lives. This unfortunate miscommunication between cultures was a pattern repeated many times throughout the West, but seldom has it been so thrillingly documented as in *El Corrido de Gregorio Cortez*.

TIME: June, 1901

PLACE: A street corner in Laredo, Texas

RUNNING TIME: 20 minutes

CAST: 15 actors, min. 6 boys, 5 girls

Gregorio Cortez	Romaldo Cortez
El Trovadore	Abuelita Piedra
Granny Stone	Sheriff Morris
Deputy Choate	Gregorio's Wife
Romaldo's Wife	Sheriff Glover
Martín Robledo	4 Posse Members

STAGE SET: a bench at down left, 3 wood blocks at mid center

PROPS: 2 sets of knitting needles, 2 socks, cooking pot, frying pan, 4 revolvers, 4 rifles, towel

EFFECTS: Sound — gun shots

MUSIC: *El Corrido de Gregorio Cortez* (should be accompanied by guitar, offstage keyboard if necessary)

COSTUMES: Gregorio and Romaldo Cortez and Martín Robledo dress as c. 1900 farm laborers — red or blue cotton shirts, denim jeans, boots; Granny Stone, Abuelita Piedra, Gregorio's Wife and Romaldo's Wife wear dark ankle-length skirt and white blouse, with Granny and Abuelita perhaps wearing a bonnet; Sheriffs and Posse Members wear gunbelts, jackets and Stetson hats in addition to dark cotton shirts, denim jeans and boots; El Trovadore wears a sombrero-style hat and a vaquero-style outfit with white shirt, brown, blue or black pegged pants and waist jacket

(LIGHTS UP RIGHT on the street corner in Laredo, on the Texas-Mexico border. At down right stands EL TROVADORE, a guitar in his hands.)

EL TROVADORE: ¡Buenas días, mis amigos! ¡Bienvenido a Laredo! People here in Laredo call me "El Trovadore" — "The Troubadour" — because I am the best singer in the whole of Texas. And of all the songs I sing, my favorite is the *corrido*, a type of Mexican folksong very popular on the Border since the 1840s. Say, you want to hear one? *(strums guitar and sings first verse of "El Corrido de Gregorio Cortez")*

EL TROVADORE: *(SINGS)*
En el condado de El Carmen
tal desgracia sucedió,
murió el Cherife Mayor,
no saben quién lo mató.

EL TROVADORE: *(speaks)*
In the County of El Carmen
Such a tragedy took place.
The Major Sheriff is dead;
No one knows who killed him.

EL TROVADORE: That is the opening verse of a great *corrido*: "El Corrido de Gregorio Cortez" — "The Ballad of Gregorio Cortez." The *corrido* is always about someone the people look up to as a hero. Sometimes a person can become a hero, even when they don't want to. Such a person was Gregorio Cortez, who lived on a small ranch in South Texas, not far from Mexico. He didn't know it right then, but on the twelfth of June, 1901, his life was going to change forever.

EL TROVADORE: *(SINGS)*
Participo esta noticia
a gente culta y honrada;
los de lista enumerad,
la suerte le sea procipia.

(LIGHTS UP LEFT on two old women, ABUELITA PIEDRA and GRANNY STONE, seated next to each other on a bench at down left; they are each knitting a sock and face the audience.)

ABUELITA PIEDRA: Mi nombre es Abuelita Piedra. My family has lived here in South Texas since 1729. When Texas joined the United States in 1846, we lost our entire ranch to the new government. They said the old Spanish and Mexican land grants were no good!

GRANNY STONE: My name is Granny Stone. I've lived along the Border since my parents came to Texas from Alabama in 1848, the year America won the Mexican War. *(nods head toward Abuelita Piedra)* Of course, some folks around here don't seem to know the war is over...and *they* lost!

ABUELITA PIEDRA: Gregorio Cortez? Sí, he was a neighbor of mine. Twenty-five years old he was, and a hard-working man with a wife and four young children. His brother, Romaldo, and Romaldo's wife lived with him.

(SHERIFF MORRIS and DEPUTY CHOATE, armed with revolvers in their holsters, enter from right and talk to El Trovadore, who shrugs his shoulders to indicate "I don't know" but points to mid center.)

GRANNY STONE: On the morning of June 12th, Sheriff Brack Morris and his deputy, Boone Choate, came to the town of Kenedy looking for a horse thief.

ABUELITA PIEDRA: The only description they had was that the thief was "a medium-sized Mexican man with a sombrero." A description that would fit any of a thousand men!

GRANNY STONE: So the Sheriff and Deputy went looking for Mexicans who'd recently acquired a new horse. Someone told them about a man who had just traded a horse for a mare — that is, a male horse for a female horse.

ABUELITA PIEDRA: Someone by the name of Gregorio Cortez.

(LIGHTS UP CENTER on GREGORIO CORTEZ, GREGORIO'S WIFE, ROMALDO CORTEZ, and ROMALDO'S WIFE at mid center; Gregorio and Romaldo Cortez sit on two blocks facing audience with their wives behind them, Gregorio's Wife holding a cooking pot and Romaldo's Wife a frying pan; Gregorio Cortez has a revolver in his belt at his side.)

GREGORIO CORTEZ: ¡Muy deliciosa! Tell me, Romaldo, are there any other wives in the whole of Texas who can cook as well as these?

ROMALDO CORTEZ: There are none better, Gregorio. We may be the best-fed men in the county!

GREGORIO'S WIFE: You are, indeed! And now you may get back to planting corn so your children have tortillas to eat this winter!

ROMALDO'S WIFE: And you can buy your wives beautiful dresses with the money left over!

(Gregorio's Wife and Romaldo's Wife laugh and exit up left; Sheriff Morris and Deputy Choate advance a few steps toward mid center and stare at Gregorio and Romaldo; Romaldo notices the Sheriff and Deputy.)

ROMALDO CORTEZ: Gregorio, mira! There is the Sheriff and his Deputy! Standing at the front gate!

GREGORIO CORTEZ: What are they doing here?

ROMALDO CORTEZ: No sé. Maybe they are looking for lunch, eh? *(chuckles)*

GREGORIO CORTEZ: Go see what they want.

(Romaldo rises and walks to the Sheriff and Deputy.)

GRANNY STONE: Now the Cortez brothers did not speak English.

ABUELITA PIEDRA: And el Cherife did not speak Spanish.

GRANNY STONE: So the Sheriff had a translator, Deputy Choate, who spoke a little bit of Spanish.

ABUELITA PIEDRA: ¡Un muy poquito! A very little bit!

GRANNY STONE: Just enough to understand the gist of things.

ABUELITA PIEDRA: Just enough to get things really mixed up.

ROMALDO CORTEZ: *(to Gregorio)* ¡Mi hermano, te quieren!

(Gregorio stands and walks to Romaldo's side.)

ABUELITA PIEDRA: Now, Romaldo had said to Gregorio—

ROMALDO CORTEZ: My brother, you are wanted!

ABUELITA PIEDRA: Meaning, "someone wants to speaks to you." But the Deputy, with his middling Spanish, thought Romaldo had meant—

DEPUTY CHOATE: *(apprehensively)* Sheriff, he's telling his brother he's a wanted man. He knows we're after him!

GRANNY STONE: So Sheriff Morris started edging toward his pistol.

SHERIFF MORRIS: *(to Deputy)* Ask him if he's recently traded for that horse over in the corral.

GRANNY STONE: In English, the word "horse" can mean either a male horse or a female horse.

ABUELITA PIEDRA: But in Spanish, the word for "horse" — *caballo* — is used only to mean a male horse. The word *yegua* is used to describe a female horse, or a mare.

GRANNY STONE: So when Deputy Choate asked if Gregorio had just traded for a horse—

DEPUTY CHOATE: *(points across stage to mid left)* Un caballo?

ABUELITA PIEDRA: Gregorio thought he meant a male horse, not the mare standing in the corral.

GREGORIO CORTEZ: No, señor. No recibí ningún caballo.

DEPUTY CHOATE: *(scratches his head in confusion)* Sheriff, he says he didn't trade for that horse.

SHERIFF MORRIS: *(to Deputy)* Well, if that's not a horse, I'm a pork chop. We'll get to the bottom of this yet. Tell them they're both under arrest. *(draws his revolver)*

GRANNY STONE: The Deputy told Gregorio and Romaldo they were under arrest, and Gregorio replied—

GREGORIO CORTEZ: *(backs up several steps)* ¡Ni puede arrestarme por nada!

ABUELITA PIEDRA: Which means, "You can't arrest me for nothing!"

GRANNY STONE: But the Deputy told the Sheriff it meant—

DEPUTY CHOATE: Watch out, Sheriff! He says, "No man can arrest me!"

SHERIFF MORRIS: We'll see about that!

(Sheriff Morris aims his revolver at Gregorio's head; Romaldo jumps in between them and is shot by Sheriff Morris; Romaldo falls to ground. SOUND: a gun shot. Gregorio draws his revolver; Sheriff Morris shoots at Gregorio and misses. SOUND: a gun shot. Gregorio shoots Sheriff. SOUND: a gun shot. Sheriff falls to ground.)

DEPUTY CHOATE: Ohmygosh! *(turns and runs toward offstage right, stopping at down right to shout at the audience)* There's a gang of bandits on the loose! They shot the Sheriff, and they're coming to kill us all! Mount up the posse! *(exits)*

(Gregorio kneels next to Romaldo; Gregorio's Wife and Romaldo's Wife enter from up left and run crying to their husbands' Romaldo's Wife applies a towel to Romaldo's face.)

GREGORIO CORTEZ: Take the children and go to my mother's house! Romaldo has been shot in the mouth and is losing blood! I will wait till night falls and take him into Kenedy to *la curandera*.

(Gregorio's Wife and Romaldo's Wife exit up left; Gregrio gets Romaldo to his feet and helps him offstage up right.)

EL TROVADORE: *(SINGS)*
Ya insortaron a Cortez
por toditito el estado,
que vivo o muerto se aprehenda
porque a varios ha matado.

ABUELITA PIEDRA: Now they have outlawed Cortez throughout the whole of the state!

GRANNY STONE: Let him be taken, dead or alive!

(FOUR POSSE MEMBERS enter from right and stride across stage to down left, scouting around with rifles and revolvers drawn, before exiting.)

GRANNY STONE: Posses formed up all over South Texas. And because the Deputy had claimed they were attacked by a whole gang of bandits from across the Mexican border, the Texas Rangers were called in.

ABUELITA PIEDRA: The Rangers...*Los Rinches*, we call them in Spanish. When they were on the hunt, they very often shot first and asked questions later. People along the Border were very frightened of what might happen.

(As Posse Members exit down left, Gregorio Cortez enters up right, cautiously, and crosses to mid center where he ducks behind one of the wood blocks.)

GRANNY STONE: That night, Gregorio got his brother to a friend's house in Kenedy. His entire family — children included — were arrested and thrown in jail as accomplices.

ABUELITA PIEDRA: The lawmen thought Gregorio would head south for Mexico. Instead, he began walking north. He walked eighty miles in forty hours, all of it through rough country. Finally, near Belmont, Texas, he came to the house of a friend, Martín Robledo and his family.

(MARTÍN ROBLEDO enters from up left and crosses to Gregorio at center.)

MARTÍN ROBLEDO: Gregorio! You will be safe in my house, for a few days at least.

GREGORIO CORTEZ: Gracias, mi amigo. *(takes off his shoes)* Con permiso.

MARTIN ROBLEDO: Sí, rest your feet. You have walked a very long way.

(Four Posse Members led by SHERIFF GLOVER enter from down left and, crouching, surround Gregorio Cortez and Martín Robledo at mid center.)

ABUELITA PIEDRA: He hadn't walked far enough. The local sheriff, Robert Glover, had a hunch the fugitive might turn up in his county, and he kept a close watch on the houses of several Mexican-Americans.

GRANNY STONE: The posse surrounded the Robledo house and, without any warning, rushed up and began firing.

(Posse Members and Sheriff Glover rise and begin firing at Gregorio Cortez and Martín Robledo. SOUND: several gun shots. Martín Robledo falls, wounded.)

GRANNY STONE: It was a fierce encounter! Sheriff Glover shot at Cortez several times but missed.

(Gregorio Cortez jumps aside to the right and shoots Sheriff Glover, who falls, dead. SOUND: a gun shot.)

GRANNY STONE: Cortez returned fire and killed the Sheriff. Then he ran off, barefoot, into the brush and hid until the shooting was over.

ABUELITA PIEDRA: Mrs. Robledo and one of the young boys — both unarmed — were wounded by the posse...who were so reckless they killed one of their own men by mistake.

(POSSE MEMBER #1 points gun at POSSE MEMBER #2, who whirls around.)

POSSE MEMBER #1: Halt!
POSSE MEMBER #2: Halt!

(Posse Member #2 shoots Posse Member #1, who falls dead. SOUND: a gun shot.)

POSSE MEMBER #2: Oops!

(Posse Members #2, 3 and 4 drag off Martín Robledo, Posse Member #1 and Sheriff Glover up left.)

GRANNY STONE: But they didn't find Gregorio Cortez. And after the posse left, he went back in the house, picked up his shoes, and headed south to the Guadalupe River.

(Gregorio Cortez retrieves his shoes and exits up right.)

ABUELITA PIEDRA: There he met a friend, who gave him a mare. Gregorio Cortez was now the most hunted man in the entire Southwest. More than eight hundred men and scores of blood-hounds were on his trail.

(Three Posse Members enter from up left and scout around the stage as El Trovadore sings.)

EL TROVADORE: *(SINGS)*
Decía Gregorio Cortez
con su pistola en la mano:
— ¡Ah, cuánto rinche montado
para un solo mexicano!

(Gregorio Cortez enters at down right, standing next to El Trovadore.)

GREGORIO CORTEZ: *(speaks, his revolver raised)*
Then said Gregorio Cortez
With his pistol in his hand,
"Ah, how many mounted Rangers
Against one lone Mexican!"

(Posse Member #2 spots Gregorio Cortez and points.)

POSSE MEMBER #2: Hey, there he is!

(Gregorio Cortez exits down right and has disappeared by the time Posse Members #3 and 4 turn.)

POSSE MEMBERS #3 & 4: Vanished into the wind!

(Posse Members resume scouting as Gregorio's Wife and Romaldo's Wife enter from down left.)

GREGORIO'S WIFE: *(speaks)*
> They let loose the bloodhounds
> So they could follow the trail,
> But trying to overtake Cortez
> Was like following a star.

ROMALDO'S WIFE: *(speaks)*
> The *Rinches* were coming;
> They seemed to fly through the air,
> Because they were going to get
> One thousand dollars in reward!

GREGORIO'S WIFE: *(speaks)*
> Then said Gregorio Cortez
> With his soul aflame—

(Gregorio Cortez enters down right.)

GREGORIO CORTEZ: *(speaks)*
> "I don't regret killing these sheriffs
> A man must defend himself!"

ROMALDO'S WIFE: *(speaks)*
> Then said Gregorio Cortez
> With his head held high—

GREGORIO CORTEZ: *(speaks)*
> "Come on, you cowardly *Rinches*,
> Don't run from just one Mexican!"

(Gregorio's Wife and Romaldo's Wife exit left; Gregorio Cortez walks around the stage boldly as Posse Members #2, 3 and 4 spy him but miss catching him.)

ABUELITA PIEDRA: For seven more days Gregorio Cortez evaded his pursuers. He rode three hundred miles over some of the roughest country in Texas, over rivers and through barbed wire.

GRANNY STONE: Once, he drove a herd of cattle to a water hole where a posse waited. They thought he was a vaquero from a nearby ranch. He drank his fill and got clean away!

POSSE MEMBER #2: The best man-trackers in the country have failed to catch him!

POSSE MEMBER #3: He moves like a ghost!

POSSE MEMBER #4: He shows no fear!

POSSE MEMBER #2: The newspapers say he's part of a large gang of bandits from Mexico!

POSSE MEMBER #3: At least eleven innocent people have been killed by over-eager lawmen who thought they were shooting at Cortez!

POSSE MEMBER #4: *(aims rifle at Posse Member #3)* Shoot first, ask questions later! *(Posse Member #3 ducks as Posse Member #4's rifle goes off. SOUND: a gun shot.)*

(Gregorio Cortez walks slowly to wood blocks at mid center and sits on one, the Posse Members moving to stand behind him.)

ABUELITA PIEDRA: On June 22nd, ten days after his ordeal began, Gregorio Cortez decided he had had enough of running. It was his twenty-sixth birthday, and he was missing his family very much. He walked into a sheep camp near the village of El Sauz a few miles from Laredo, and he waited for the posse to arrive.

GRANNY STONE: When the posse came to the camp, they didn't know Cortez was there. So he sent a man out to tell them.

GREGORIO CORTEZ: *(stands, puts down his revolver)* Go let the *Rinches* know they can arrest me. They can take me only because I'm willing — not any other way.

(Posse Members lead Gregorio Cortez down center, where he stands facing audience; LIGHTS FADE DOWN TO SPOT-LIGHT on Gregorio Cortez.)

ABUELITA PIEDRA: After several trials, Gregorio Cortez was found not guilty of killing Sheriff Morris. He was, however, convicted of killing Sheriff Glover and sentenced to spend the rest of his life in prison.

GRANNY STONE: But in 1913, Gregorio Cortez was granted a pardon by the Governor of Texas and was released. He was thirty-eight years old and had spent nearly one-third of his life in jail. All because he didn't speak good English.

ABUELITA PIEDRA: All because the translator spoke bad Spanish.

GRANNY STONE: All because he had traded a mare for a horse.

ABUELITA PIEDRA: All because men let their guns speak —
instead of their reason.
GRANNY STONE: Aye, such is life!
ABUELITA PIEDRA: ¡Ay, asi es la vida!

(LIGHTS FADE UP FULL as entire cast gathers at down center to sing.)

ENTIRE CAST: *(SING)*
Ya con ésta me despido
a la sombra de un ciprés;
aquí se acaba el corrido
de don Gregorio Cortez.

Now with this I say farewell
In the shade of a cypress tree;
This is the end of the ballad
of Don Gregorio Cortez.
ENTIRE CAST: *(speaks)*
¡Viva el corrido!

(LIGHTS OUT.)

THE END

El Corrido de Gregorio Cortez
(traditional, arranged by L.E. McCullough)

FANDANGO!

Though life for early settlers in the Wild West was usually very hard, there were occasional social events where people could relax and have fun. These "shindigs" or "fandangos" often brought together many cultures; the common denominator of music and dance made folks temporarily forget their differences as everyone contributed to the entertainment with a story or a song. In this play two characters are based on real people. Born a slave in Tennessee, Nat Love (1854-1907) came West at age 15 and achieved fame as a cowboy, Army scout and rodeo rider. "Stagecoach" Mary Fields (1833-1914), another African-American native of Tennessee, was likewise a legend in her lifetime — a six-foot-four, two hundred-pound freight wagon driver who was the second American woman to carry a U.S. mail route.

TIME: March, 1887

PLACE: A prospector's cabin in the Rocky Mountains of Montana

RUNNING TIME: 30 minutes

CAST: 24 actors, min. 10 boys, 10 girls

Hard Tack Horton	Captain Crandall
Señor Garcia	Señora Garcia
4 Señoritas	2 Vaqueros
El Ciego, the Blind Fiddler	La Gitana, the Gypsy Guitarist
Trapper Boulez, a Scout	Patrick Clancy, a Logger
Nat Love, a Cowboy	2 Papago Indians
Hiram Brannan, Father	Margaret Brannan, Mother
Sylvia Brannan, Daughter	Judith Brannan, Daughter
2 Cowboys	Stagecoach Mary Fields

STAGE SET: a bench at mid center

PROPS: a boot, bandana, axe, flower

EFFECTS: Sound — winter wind howling; loud door knocking

MUSIC: *La Encantadora*; *Un, Deux, Trois*; *Weevily Wheat*; *Dime Sí, Sí, Sí*; *When I Was a Cowboy*; *The Woodsman's Alphabet*; *Poor Wayfaring Stranger*; *Song of Good Luck*; *The Cowboy's Dream*

COSTUMES: All characters dress according to occupation — Hard Tack Horton dresses as a prospector, Captain Crandall wears a cavalry officer's uniform, Nat Love as a typical cowboy, etc.; the Garcias and the Señoritas should wear somewhat fancy and colorful Mexican-style fiesta clothes

PERFORMANCE NOTES: Live music is not necessary, but it certainly makes things a lot livelier — just as they would be at a genuine fandango. The fiddler and guitarist should accompany the singers whenever possible. Musicians can sit on bench throughout, and other characters can join them after they have performed their song at center stage. To further emphasize the fiesta quality of the fandango, a food table can be set up at mid right, and piñatas and other decorations can be hung around left and center stage.

(LIGHTS UP RIGHT. At down right is the interior of a prospector's cabin in the Rocky Mountains of Montana; two men with blankets wrapped around them, HARD TACK HORTON and CAPTAIN CRANDALL, sit cross-legged facing the audience, staring at a boot in front of them. SOUND: winter wind howling offstage.)

HARD TACK HORTON: The owls. Those dadblasted white owls! I knew it was gonna be a bad winter when I saw the white owls last September. Never did see a white owl before, not in forty years of prospecting the West. The Cheyenne say a white owl is a very bad sign. "Heap snow coming, very cold." But did Hard Tack Horton listen to an old Indian legend that's been around for a thousand years! Nosireee! He took the advice of some city newspaper meteorologist who said this winter will be the mildest in ten years. Meteorologist! Sounds like some quack sawbones who takes out your appendix when all you went in for was a toothache!

CAPTAIN CRANDALL: *(sits up straight)* At ease, Horton! Time to stop gibbering and take stock of the situation. It is the first of March, 1887. Snow has been falling for two weeks. I — Captain Christopher Crandall, U.S. Sixth Cavalry — am stranded with a local prospector in a cabin high atop Scapegoat Mountain, nine thousand one hundred eighty-five feet above sea level, just west of the Continental Divide in the great Rocky Mountains of Montana. That is all! *(salutes)*

HARD TACK HORTON: You left out the part about how our food is gone and we've burnt every stick of furniture but the walls.

CAPTAIN CRANDALL: I must needs remind you, soldier, that desertion is a court-martial offense! Now, shine that boot and prepare for troop inspection!

HARD TACK HORTON: First off, Captain, I ain't no dadblasted soldier. Never was, never will be! Second, we'll be *eating* that boot in about an hour. And then, maybe each other. Reminds me of the time back in '47 when this fella named Donner asked me to lead his caravan—

CAPTAIN CRANDALL: *(puts hands over his ears)* Oh, please, please, *please*! Not another one of your idiot stories about the old days in the Wild West!

HARD TACK HORTON: You have a better idea how to pass the

time in this blizzard? And keep your mind off chewing my ankles? Mmmm...Ankles. Did I say *ankles*? Well, let me tell you about the prettiest set of female ankles I ever saw. It was in Tucson, Arizona Territory, on the fifth of May, 1872. I was on my way to Colorado, but it being a holiday in those parts, I ended up with an invite to come to one of the big haciendas — and enjoy a first-class *fandango*!

(LIGHTS DOWN RIGHT; LIGHTS UP CENTER AND LEFT. MUSIC: "La Encantadora" played on violin and guitar. At mid center [perhaps sitting on bench] EL CIEGO plays his violin and LA GITANA plays her guitar as SEÑOR GARCIA, SEÑORITA GARCIA, FOUR SEÑORITAS, TRAPPER BOULEZ and NAT LOVE enter from left and cross to down center; Señor and Señora Garcia enter in a stately fashion, arm-in-arm; the Four Señoritas enter dancing briskly to the instrumental music, with Trapper Boulez and Nat Love skipping along behind them. When all are at center stage, MUSIC STOPS.)

SEÑOR GARCIA: Damas y caballeros, amigos y amigas! On behalf of La Familia Garcia, I welcome you to our celebration of El Cinco de Mayo!

SEÑORA GARCIA: It was ten years ago today at the Battle of Puebla that General Ignacio Zaragosa and the Army of Free Mexico defeated the invading French army of Napoleon the Third. The French, despite their superior numbers and training, lost over a thousand men; Zaragosa lost only eighty-six.

SEÑOR GARCIA: If the French had won, they would have conquered all of Mexico and then turned north to aid the Confederacy in the American Civil War.

SEÑORA GARCIA: So this holiday we celebrate is a holiday of freedom. A holiday for the democracy that rules the United States and now Mexico as well! ¡Viva Cinco de Mayo!

EVERYONE EXCEPT TRAPPER BOULEZ: ¡Viva Cinco de Mayo!

(Trapper Boulez, visibly angry, steps up to Señor Garcia.)

TRAPPER BOULEZ: Monsieur! *I*, Trapper Boulez, am French — from New Orleans, Louisiana — and I take somewhat an exception to your remarks. Begging your pardon most sincerely, it is now my duty to avenge ze honor of my nation! I request you to duel with me at once! *(bows)*

(Four Señoritas gasp and wail.)

SEÑOR GARCIA: Very well, Señor Trapper. But *I* choose the weapons. Songs at ten paces!

TRAPPER BOULEZ: D'accord! Here is a song I heard on the bayou as a petit garçon — "Un, Deux, Trois."

(Trapper Boulez faces audience and sings. MUSIC: "Un, Deux, Trois.")

TRAPPER BOULEZ: *(SINGS)*
    Un, deux, trois,
    Caroline qui fais comme ça, ma chère?
    Un, deux, trois,
    Caroline qui fais comme ça, ma chère?
    Maman dit oui, papa dit non,
    Celui mo lais, celui mo prends.
    Maman dit oui, papa dit non,
    Celui mo lais, celui mo prends.

TRAPPER BOULEZ & FOUR SEÑORITAS: *(SING)*
    One, two, three,
    Caroline, what is the matter with you, my dear?
    One, two, three,
    Caroline, what is the matter with you, my dear?
    Mama says yes, papa says no,
    It is he I wish, it is he I'll have.
    Mama says yes, papa says no,
    It is he I wish, it is he I'll have.

(Trapper Boulez and Señor Garcia bow to each other.)

SEÑOR GARCIA: ¡Muy bien! You have indeed proved yourself a powerful singer. Your honor is upheld!

TRAPPER BOULEZ: Laissez les bons temps roulet! Let the good times roll!

(NAT LOVE exuberantly strides to center stage, embracing Señoritas and shaking hands with Trapper Boulez and Señor and Señora Garcia.)

NAT LOVE: Whoo-ee! Hang me up for bear meat and send my hide to Texas! If this isn't the best fandango in Arizona, then I am a lop-eared mud hen! *(laughs)*

SEÑORA GARCIA: ¡Mira! Here is the famous cowboy Nat Love!

NAT LOVE: Howdy, all! I just finished a cattle drive up to Dodge City, and I had me some adventures the like you've never heard!

(Nat Love faces audience and sings. MUSIC: "When I Was a Cowboy.")

NAT LOVE: *(SINGS)*
When I was a cowboy out on the Western plains,
When I was a cowboy out on the Western plains,
I made a million dollars driving a cattle train.
Coma-cow-cow-yippie-yippie
Cow-cow-yippie-ay-a

Oh the hardest battle was ever on Bunker Hill,
Oh the hardest battle was ever on Bunker Hill,
When me and a bunch of cowboys run into Buffalo Bill.

OTHERS: *(SING)*
Coma-cow-cow-yippie-yippie
Cow-cow-yippie-ay-a

NAT LOVE: *(SINGS)*
Oh the hardest battle was ever on the Western plains,
Oh the hardest battle was ever on the Western plains,
When me and a bunch of cowboys run into Jesse James.

OTHERS: *(SING)*
Coma-cow-cow-yippie-yippie
Cow-cow-yippie-ay-a

NAT LOVE: *(SINGS)*
When me and a bunch of cowboys run into Jesse James,
When me and a bunch of cowboys run into Jesse James,
The bullets were a-falling just like a shower of rain.

OTHERS: *(SING)*
Coma-cow-cow-yippie-yippie
Cow-cow-yippie-ay-a

NAT LOVE: *(speaks)* Now, the boys caught up with an outlaw on the outskirts of town. All around the man's house, the horses were a-walking, and the forty-fives were a-talking. After awhile, they sent their best regards to the man's house.

NAT LOVE: *(SINGS)*
If your house catches on fire, and there ain't no water round,
If your house catches on fire, and there ain't no water round,
Throw your jelly out the window, let the doggone shack burn
   down.

OTHERS: *(SING)*
Coma-cow-cow-yippie-yippie
Cow-cow-yippie-ay-a

(All applaud; PATRICK CLANCY enters from left, carrying an axe and wiping his face with a bandana as he crosses to center.)

PATRICK CLANCY: Saints above, I'm nearly killed altogether with this terrible heat!

NAT LOVE: Why, it's my old pal Patrick Clancy, the logger! What brings you to these parts? There's no trees for you to cut in this desert!

PATRICK CLANCY: Well now, if it's not one thing, it's the other. But do you know, back in the old days, they say it was hot like this in Ireland.

TRAPPER BOULEZ: And how hot was it?

PATRICK CLANCY: Why, it was so hot, it would curl the horns of a cow! And the rivers got so hot, they boiled over and everyone ate broiled fish for a year! And though people say St. Patrick drove the snakes out of Ireland with a mighty staff, the truth is it was so hot the snakes stuck to his feet and he carried them out on his shoes!

(All laugh.)

SEÑOR GARCIA: Before you go back to the North Woods, will you sing a song, por favor?

PATRICK CLANCY: I will, indeed. It is called "The Woodsman's Alphabet."

(Patrick Clancy faces audience and sings. MUSIC: "The Woodsman's Alphabet.")

PATRICK CLANCY: *(SINGS)*
A is for the Axes, we very well know

B is for the Boys that use them also
C is for Chopping, which we did begin
D is for Danger we always are in

OTHERS: *(SING)*

Oh, merry, oh, merry, oh, merry are we
No mortals on earth are as happy as we
Sing hi derry, ho derry, hi derry dee
The shantyman swings and the timber flies free

PATRICK CLANCY: *(SINGS)*

E is for Echo that through the woods rang
F is for Foreman that forwards our gang
G is for Grindstone we often did turn
H is for the Handle so smoothernly worn

OTHERS: *(SING)*

Oh, merry, oh, merry, oh, merry are we
No mortals on earth are as happy as we
Sing hi derry, ho derry, hi derry dee
The shantyman swings and the timber flies free

PATRICK CLANCY: *(SINGS)*

I is for Iron that marketh our pine
J is for Joyvellers we leaveth behind
K is for the Keen edge our axes did keep
L is for Lice that keep us from sleep

OTHERS: *(SING)*

Oh, merry, oh, merry, oh, merry are we
No mortals on earth are as happy as we
Sing hi derry, ho derry, hi derry dee
The shantyman swings and the timber flies free

PATRICK CLANCY: *(SINGS)*

M is the Moss we use in our camps
N is for the Needle that mendeth our pants
O is for the Owl that hootheth at night
P if for the Pine we always fell right

OTHERS: *(SING)*

Oh, merry, oh, merry, oh, merry are we
No mortals on earth are as happy as we
Sing hi derry, ho derry, hi derry dee
The shantyman swings and the timber flies free

PATRICK CLANCY: *(SINGS)*

    Q is for Quarreling we never allow

    R is for the River where our logs they did flow

    S if for the Sled so stout and so strong

    T is for the Team that scooted them along

OTHERS: *(SING)*

    Oh, merry, oh, merry, oh, merry are we

    No mortals on earth are as happy as we

    Sing hi derry, ho derry, hi derry dee

    The shantyman swings and the timber flies free

PATRICK CLANCY: *(SINGS)*

    U is for the Use we put our teams to

    V is for the Valley we cut our roads through

    W is for the Woods we left in the spring

    X is for nothing a logger can't sing

    Y is for the Yells when the timber comes down

    Z is for the Zither and dances in town

    Now you have heard all I'm going to rhyme

    So gather your axes and up the tree climb

OTHERS: *(SING)*

    Oh, merry, oh, merry, oh, merry are we

    No mortals on earth are as happy as we

    Sing hi derry, ho derry, hi derry dee

    The shantyman swings and the timber flies free

(All applaud; TWO VAQUEROS enter from left and cross to center; VAQUERO #1 takes the hand of SEÑORITA #1.)

SEÑORA GARCIA: Here come two vaqueros from El Rancho Grande! ¡Bienvenido, muchachos! Help yourselves to the enchiladadas and tamales!

VAQUERO #2: Gracias, señora. But we have not ridden all this way for food. We have come because my brother, Juan, is in love!

VAQUERO #1: Librada, you are the mistress of my heart! ¡Te amo! I love you!

SEÑORITA #1: *(drops his hand, turns away)* You vaqueros always talk of love! ¡No te creo! I do not believe you!

VAQUERO #1: Then, I will prove it with a song!

(Two Vaqueros face Señorita #1 and sing to her. MUSIC: "Dime Sí, Sí, Sí.")

TWO VAQUEROS: *(SING)*
 Acabo de llegar de la majada,
 de cueros traigo lleno un carretón,
 se los traigo a regalar a mi Librada,
 la dueña de mi corazón.

OTHERS: *(SING)*
 Dime sí, sí, sí, dime no, no, no,
 aguardiente traía pero ya se me acabó.
 Dime sí, sí, sí, dime no, no, no,
 aguardiente traía pero ya se me acabó.

TWO VAQUEROS: *(SING)*
 I have just arrived from the sheep pens,
 I am bringing in a wagon full of hides;
 I have brought them as a gift to my Librada,
 The mistress of my heart.

OTHERS: *(SING)*
 Tell me yes, yes, yes; tell me no, no, no;
 I brought some spirits with me, but now they are all gone.
 Tell me yes, yes, yes; tell me no, no, no;
 I brought some spirits with me, but now they are all gone.

(All applaud; Vaquero #1 kneels and offers her a flower.)

VAQUERO #1: My dearest Librada! Will you marry me?
SEÑORITA #1: I will think about it.
VAQUERO #2: And let him know by the end of the fandango?
SEÑORITA #1: Tal vez sí...tal vez no! *(takes flower in her mouth and strides away right)*
VAQUERO #1: ¡Mi corazón! *(swoons, is caught by Vaquero #2 and dragged away left)*

(HIRAM BRANNAN, MARGARET BRANNAN, SYLVIA BRANNAN and JUDITH BRANNAN enter from left and cross wearily to center, assisted by TWO PAPAGO INDIANS.)

NAT LOVE: Why, these folks look like they've been rode hard and put up wet!

PATRICK CLANCY: If they came through the Sonora Desert, sure, it's a wonder they're alive at all!

HIRAM BRANNAN: My name is Hiram Brannan. This is my wife, Margaret, and our daughters Sylvia and Judith.

MARGARET BRANNAN: We are members of the Church of Jesus Christ of Latter-day Saints — often called Mormons by the gentile peoples.

SYLVIA BRANNAN: We have come from Utah to start a new settlement in Arizona, but our wagon train became lost in the desert.

JUDITH BRANNAN: We are the only surivivors. And we would not be alive if it were not for the kindness of these Papago Indians who rescued us.

HIRAM BRANNAN: Let us sing a hymn of thanks for our salvation.

(The Brannans face audience and sing. MUSIC: "Poor Wayfaring Stranger.")

THE BRANNANS: *(SING)*
I'm just a poor, wayfaring stranger
A-traveling through this world of woe;
But there's no sickness, toil nor danger
In that bright world to which I go.

I'm going there to meet my father,
I'm going there no more to roam,
I'm just a-going over Jordan,
I'm just a-going over home.

I know dark clouds will gather round me;
I know my way is rough and steep.
But beauteous fields lie just beyond me,
Where souls redeemed their vigil keep.

BRANNANS & OTHERS: *(SING)*
I'm going there to meet my mother,
She said she'd meet me when I come;
I'm just a-going over Jordan,
I'm just a-going over home.

(All applaud; the Brannans are helped to the bench by the Papago Indians.)

SEÑORA GARCIA: You are welcome here. Nuestro casa es sus casa.

(TWO COWBOYS enter from left and saunter to center.)

COWBOY #1: Greetings, all! If we look like a couple of grayback cowpunchers from the Circle D Ranch down by Nogales, it's because we are!

COWBOY #2: We heard there was a fandango tonight! Looks like we weren't far wrong!

COWBOY #1: Then why isn't anybody dancing?

COWBOY #2: Fiddler, strike up the band and let's make the calico crack!

(A four-couple square dance forms with Four Señoritas dancing with Two Cowboys and Two Vaqueros while others clap along and sing; El Ciego and La Gitana play music. MUSIC: "Weevily Wheat.")

GARCIAS, NAT LOVE, TRAPPER BOULEZ,
PATRICK CLANCY: *(SING)*

Oh, Charley he's a nice young man
Charley he's a dandy;
Every time he goes to town
He brings the girls some candy.

BRANNANS & INDIANS: *(SING)*

Oh, I won't have none of your weevily wheat,
I won't have none of your barley,
It'll take some flour and a half an hour
To bake a cake for Charley.

GARCIAS, NAT LOVE, TRAPPER BOULEZ,
PATRICK CLANCY: *(SING)*

Charley here and Charley there
And Charley over the ocean,
Charley he'll come back some day
If he doesn't change his notion.

BRANNANS & INDIANS: *(SING)*

Oh, I won't have none of your weevily wheat,
I won't have none of your barley,
It'll take some flour and a half an hour
To bake a cake for Charley.

GARCIAS, NAT LOVE, TRAPPER BOULEZ,

PATRICK CLANCY: *(SING)*
>Over the hill to feed my sheep
>And over the river to Charley;
>Over the hill to feed my sheep
>On buckwheat cakes and barley.

BRANNANS & INDIANS: *(SING)*
>Oh, I won't have none of your weevily wheat,
>I won't have none of your barley,
>It'll take some flour and a half an hour
>To bake a cake for Charley.

(Dance ends; all applaud and holler.)

SEÑOR GARCIA: Amigos y amigas, it is getting late. Does anyone have any more songs to sing?

PAPAGO INDIAN #1: For those who must ride far, we offer a Song of Good Luck.

PAPAGO INDIAN #2: May the Great Spirit hear our prayer!

(Papago Indians #1 & 2 sing. MUSIC: "Song of Good Luck.")

PAPAGO INDIANS #1 & 2: *(SING)*
>Hai-ya, hai-ya, hai-ya-eh
>O-ha-le-hai-ya, o-ha-le

PAPAGO INDIAN #1: *(SINGS)*
>In the great night my heart will go out,
>Toward me the darkness comes rattling

PAPAGO INDIAN #2: *(SINGS)*
>At the edge of the world it is growing light,
>Up rears the dawn spreading its fingers over the night.

ENTIRE CAST: *(SING)*
>Hai-ya, hai-ya, hai-ya-eh
>O-ha-le-hai-ya, o-ha-le

(All applaud; Two Cowboys step forward to center.)

COWBOY #1: Folks, this has been a right bully fandango…

COWBOY #2: We're thankful for the friendship you've shared.

COWBOY #1: So excuse us for gettin' sorta sentimental…

COWBOY #2: But we'd like to leave you with this little air.

(Cowboys #1 & 2 sing. MUSIC: "The Cowboy's Dream.")

COWBOYS #1 & 2: *(SING)*
>When I think of that last great round-up
>On the eve of eternity's dawn,
>I think of the host of cowboys
>That have been with us here and have gone.

ENTIRE CAST: *(SING)*
>Roll on, roll on,
>Roll on, little dogies, roll on, roll on;
>Roll on, roll on,
>Roll on, little dogies, roll on.

COWBOYS #1 & 2: *(SING)*
>I think of those big-hearted fellows
>Who'll divide with you blanket and bread
>With a piece of stray beef well roasted
>And charge for it never a red.

>The trail to green pastures, though narrow,
>Leads straight to the home in the sky,
>To the headquarters ranch of the Father
>In the land of the sweet by-and-by.

ENTIRE CAST: *(SING)*
>Roll on, roll on,
>Roll on, little dogies, roll on, roll on;
>Roll on, roll on,
>Roll on, little dogies, roll on.

COWBOYS #1 & 2: *(SING)*
>The Inspector will stand at the gateway
>Where the herd, one and all, must go by;
>And the round-up by the angels in judgment
>Must pass 'neath His all-seeing eye.

>No maverick or slick will be tallied
>In that great book of life in His home,
>For he knows all the brands and the earmarks
>That down through all ages have come.

ENTIRE CAST: *(SING)*
>Roll on, roll on,
>Roll on, little dogies, roll on, roll on;
>Roll on, roll on,
>Roll on, little dogies, roll on.

COWBOYS #1 & 2: *(SING)*
>But I trust in that last great round-up
>When the Rider shall cut the big herd,

That the cowboy will be represented
In the earmark and brand of the Lord.

To be shipped to that bright, mystic region,
Over there in green pastures to lie,
And be led by the crystal still waters
To the home in the sweet by-and-by.

ENTIRE CAST: *(SING)*
Roll on, roll on,
Roll on, little dogies, roll on, roll on;
Roll on, roll on,
Roll on, little dogies, roll on.

(SOUND: loud door knocking offstage. LIGHTS CENTER AND LEFT OUT; LIGHTS UP RIGHT on Horton and Crandall still sitting on floor.)

STAGECOACH MARY FIELDS: *(offstage right)* Anybody in there? *(SOUND: door knocking)* It's too cold to be standing out here if nobody's in there!

(STAGECOACH MARY FIELDS enters from right; Horton and Crandall scramble to their feet.)

HARD TACK HORTON: Why, great jumping California horny toads, it's Stagecoach Mary Fields! We're saved, Captain, we're saved!

STAGECOACH MARY FIELDS: But you must have lost your brains along the way up here! Don't you know there's a blizzard going on? Why, so many cattle and sheep have frozen to death this winter, they're calling it "the Great Die-up of '87"!

CAPTAIN CRANDALL: How did you find us? How did you get through in this weather?

STAGECOACH MARY FIELDS: Captain, I've been delivering the U.S. mail in Western Montana for eight years, and I've never missed a day yet. As far as knowing where you were, I just thought of the dumbest place in the whole world for a crazy prospector and a pony soldier to head — and this was it! Now, come on! I've got more mail to deliver!

(Stagecoach Mary Fields exits right, Crandall and Horton following her, when Crandall stops and turns to Horton.)

CAPTAIN CRANDALL: One moment, Horton.
HARD TACK HORTON: Yes, Captain.

CAPTAIN CRANDALL: In all that fandango business, I never heard anything about you. Did all that really happen? Or did you just make it up to keep me from eating that boot?

HARD TACK HORTON: Now, Captain. Don't begrudge an old prospector his youthful memories. Course, it happened!

(He claps Captain on back, as Captain exits right, then turns to the audience.)

HARD TACK HORTON: Course, it *didn't* happen! But it *should* have! And maybe if you're lucky, someday you'll be at a fandango just like it! Roll on, little dogies, roll on! *(exits right)*

(MUSIC UP: "La Encantadora" played one time through. LIGHTS OUT.)

THE END

La Encantadora (The Enchantress)
by L.E. McCullough

© L.E. McCullough 1997

Un, Deux, Trois
(traditional, arranged by L.E. McCullough)

Un, deux, trois, Car- o- line qui fais com- me ça, ma chère?

Un, deux, trois, Car- o- line qui fais com- me ça, ma chère?

Ma- man dit oui, pa- pa dit non, ce- lui mo lais, ce- lui mo prends.

Ma- man dit oui, pa- pa dit non, ce- lui mo lais, ce- lui mo prends.

When I Was a Cowboy
(traditional, arranged by L.E. McCullough)

When I was a cow- boy out on the Wes- tern plains,

When I was a cow- boy out on the Wes- tern plains,

I made a mil- lion dol- lars dri- ving a cat- tle

train. Com-a- cow-cow- yip- pie- yip- pie cow-cow- yip- pie- ay- a

Weevily Wheat
(traditional, arranged by L.E. McCullough)

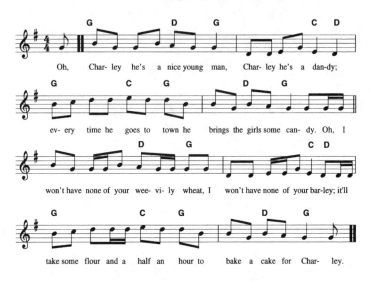

Oh, Char- ley he's a nice young man, Char- ley he's a dan- dy;

ev- ery time he goes to town he brings the girls some can- dy. Oh, I

won't have none of your wee- vi- ly wheat, I won't have none of your bar- ley; it'll

take some flour and a half an hour to bake a cake for Char- ley.

Song of Good Luck
(words & music: L.E. McCullough)

Hai- ya, hai- ya, hai- ya- eh; O- ha- le- hai- ya, o- ha-

le. In the great night my heart will go out; toward me the

dark- ness comes ratt- ling. At the edge of the world it is grow- ing light,

up rears the dawn sprea- ding its fin- gers o- ver the night.

Hai- ya, hai- ya, hai- ya- eh; O- ha- le- hai- ya, o- ha- le

Dime Sí, Sí, Sí
(traditional, arranged by L.E. McCullough)

A- ca- bo de lle- gar de la ma- ja- da, de

cue- ros trai- go lle- no_un ca- rre- tón, se los

trai- go_a re- ga- lar a mi Lib- ra- da, la

due- ña de mi co- ra- zón. Di- me sí, sí, sí, di- me

no, no, no, a- guar- dien- te tra- í- a pe- ro

ya se me_a- ca- bó. Di- me sí, sí, sí, di- me

no, no, no, a- guar- dien- te tra- í- a pe- ro ya se me_a- ca- bó.

The Woodsman's Alphabet
(traditional, arranged by L.E. McCullough)

A is for Ax- es, we ve- ry well know; B is for the Boys— that use them al- so; C is for Chop-ping, which we did be- gin D is for Dan- ger we al- ways are in. Oh, mer- ry, oh, mer- ry, oh, mer-ry are we; no mor- tals on earth are as hap- py as we; Sing hi der- ry, ho der- ry, hi der- ry dee; the shan- ty- man swings and the tim- ber flies free.

Poor Wayfaring Stranger
(traditional, arranged by L.E. McCullough)

I'm just a poor, way- far- ing stran- ger a- tra- vel- ing through this world of woe; But there's no sick- ness, toil nor dan- ger in that bright world to which I go. I'm go- ing there to meet my fa- ther, I'm go- ing there no more to roam; I'm just a- go- ing o- ver Jor- dan, I'm just a- go- ing o- ver home.

The Cowboy's Dream
(traditional, arranged by L.E. McCullough)

When I think of that la—st great round-up on the eve of e- ter- ni- ty's dawn, I think of the host —— of cow-boys that have been with us here and have gone. Roll on, roll on, roll on, lit- tle do- gies, roll on, roll on; Roll on, roll on, roll on, lit- tle do- gies, roll on.

GREASEPAINT AND GINTHONS:
THE MEDICINE SHOW COMES TO TOWN

For many folks who lived in the vast, scarcely populated expanses of the West during the late 1800s, the appearance in town of a traveling medicine show was a welcome entertainment. The shows sold "patent" medicines — homemade concoctions that had little real medicinal value or content. The "doctor" who spoke to the crowds was often an actor, and the medicine shows used musicians, singers and occasionally dancers and jugglers to attract crowds to hear the doctor's "pitch." Hobos were also a part of the social landscape of the West. During the late 1800s the United States economy suffered many recessions called "panics"; hundreds of thousands of people lost their jobs and took to wandering around the country looking for temporary work along the way, and a hobo "culture" with its own songs and folklore was created.

TIME: Sometime in the 1880s

PLACE: A little bitty town somewhere West of the Pecos

RUNNING TIME: 30 minutes

CAST: 14 actors, 6 boys, 3 girls

Ben	Hungry Hobo/Georgia Peach
Aunt Beatrice	Dr. Mortimer Q. Peach
Dusty Peach	Rusty Peach
6 Townsfolk	2 Gunslingers

STAGE SET: a wide bench at down right; easel at down left; scrim painted to resemble circus tent exterior at mid center with a wooden crate or box sitting to the right

PROPS: 3 pound cakes, cake tray, harmonica, sling shot, placard, easel, bucket, a handful of quarters, six-shooter, cloth, container of stage makeup (white greasepaint and burnt cork), saddle bag, a pair of boots, Stetson hat, long worm (rubber worm), medicine bottle, 2 cases of medicine bottles

EFFECTS: Sound — fire crackers, clanking chains, whiplash, loud rips and tears

MUSIC: *The Big Rock Candy Mountains*, *The Garden Where the Praties Grow*, *Long, Long Ago*, *For He's a Jolly Good Fellow*

COSTUMES: Ben, Townsfolk, Aunt Beatrice, Gunslingers wear basic Western rural clothes of the 1880s; Medicine Show characters dress a bit fancier, with Dr. Peach wearing a stovepipe or otherwise large hat and fancy frock coat; Hungry Hobo dresses in old jeans, plaid shirt, mashed-up hat, fake beard or wig

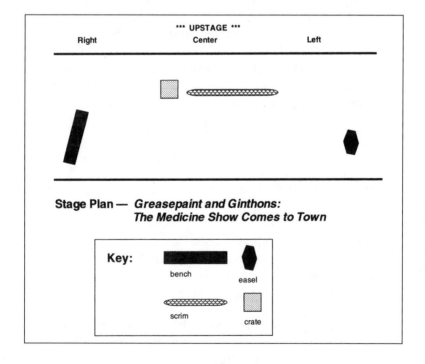

(LIGHTS UP FULL. At down right is a bench on which three pound cakes in a tray are sitting. A HUNGRY HOBO enters from left, strolling toward center stage, tooting a harmonica and singing. MUSIC: "The Big Rock Candy Mountains.")

HUNGRY HOBO: *(SINGS)*
One evening as the sun went down,
And the jungle fires were burning.
Down the track came a hobo hamming
And he said, "Boys, I'm not returning.
I'm headed for a land that's far away
Beside the crystal fountains.
I'll see you all this coming fall
In the Big Rock Candy Mountains!"

(AUNT BEATRICE and BEN enter from right and stand at down right.)

AUNT BEATRICE: Now, Benjamin, I just baked these three strawberry short cakes. Are you *sure* I can trust you to watch them for an hour?

BEN: Of course, Aunt Beatrice. I'll guard them with my life!

AUNT BEATRICE: That's what you said the last time. Do you remember what happened?

BEN: Yes, maam. The Thompson twins came over, and...and, well, we played a little hide-and-seek.

AUNT BEATRICE: Hide-and-seek, indeed! *They* hid the cakes, and *I'm* still seeking them! Well, if you want to go to the ice cream social on Saturday, you have to prove you can be responsible! After all, you're almost ten years old. *(exits right)*

BEN: I won't fail, Aunt Beatrice! *(to audience)* By jiminy, I *won't* fail, either! Wild horses couldn't drag me away from these cakes! Nor ferocious grizzly bears, nor saber-tooth wildcats, nor a herd of stampeding buffalo and bloodthirsty desperados! *(folds arms across his chest)* No sir!

(Hungry Hobo plays a snippet of melody to "The Big Rock Candy Mountains" and strolls up to Ben.)

HUNGRY HOBO: Howdy there, sonny. Fine and glorious day!

BEN: *(shrinks back to stand protectively in front of cakes)* You can't have a bite, not a crumb, not a morsel!

HUNGRY HOBO: *(chuckles)* Begging your pardon, my young sir, but to what are you referring?

BEN: Ummm, errr, gosh, uhhh, my sling shot! *(pulls sling shot from his waist and holds it up)* You can't eat my sling shot!

HUNGRY HOBO: Well now, I don't know as if I have an appetite for a sling shot.

BEN: Whew! That's good. Cause the leather is old and pretty tough.

HUNGRY HOBO: But I am fairly tempted by those strawberry short cakes on that bench behind you.

BEN: Those? Oh, they're not strawberry short cakes! They're, ummm, errr, gosh, uhhh, they're croquet balls!

HUNGRY HOBO: *(walks around Ben and peers at the cakes)* That so? *(sniffs cakes)* They sure smell like strawberry short cakes.

BEN: *(brandishes sling shot)* Well, they're not! And even if they were, you couldn't have them! My Aunt Beatrice said so!

HUNGRY HOBO: Sonny, I haven't had a bite to eat in three days. I'm the hungriest hobo West of the Pecos!

BEN: I'm sorry, sir. But I'll get in big trouble.

HUNGRY HOBO: Get in trouble for doing a good deed? What sort of cockamamie notion is that? Tell you what I'll do. I'll riddle you for them.

BEN: Riddle me for them?

HUNGRY HOBO: You're a smart young fellow, aren't you?

BEN: *(swells up with pride)* Some folks say so!

HUNGRY HOBO: I'll give you three riddles. If you guess 'em, I'll go away and not come back. If you miss 'em, I get the cakes!

BEN: Sounds fair enough!

HUNGRY HOBO: Preponderantly fair, my boy, preponderantly fair. Now, here's the first riddle. What happens to little girls who swallow bullets?

BEN: Ummm, errr, gosh, uhhh...I don't know.

HUNGRY HOBO: Their hair grows out in bangs! Bangs, get it! *(laughs, picks up a cake)* Second riddle. What's round as a hoop, deep as a cup, and all the king's horses can't pull it up?

BEN: Ummm, errr, gosh, uhhh...I don't know.

HUNGRY HOBO: A well. *(laughs, picks up second cake)* Thought you were a smart young fellow!

BEN: I am!

HUNGRY HOBO: Then try this last riddle. If you guess it, I'll give you the other two cakes back. Listen closely. What is it that takes in green, comes out white and then turns yellow?

BEN: Ummm, errr, gosh, uhhh...could you say that again?

HUNGRY HOBO: Stumped, aren't you, sonny? It's a cow. Grass is green, milk is white, butter is yellow. I'll thank you to hand me that third cake.

(Ben hands him the third cake and tray, and Hungry Hobo strolls off left with tray and cakes, singing. MUSIC: chorus to "The Big Rock Candy Mountains.")

HUNGRY HOBO: *(SINGS)*
In the Big Rock Candy Mountains
There's a land that's fair and bright,
Where the handouts grow on bushes,
And you sleep out every night.
Where the boxcars all are empty,
And the sun shines every day.
O, the birds and the bees and the peppermint trees,
The fudge cake springs where the whang doodle sings
In the Big Rock Candy Mountains.

BEN: Now, I'm really in trouble! Aunt Beatrice will tan my hide when she finds out I let that hungry hobo have the cakes! Of course, I could tell her a big whopper of a fib! That a gang of outlaws came and pulled out their six-shooters and made me give them the cakes! Naw...I can't lie...Reckon there's only one thing left to do...I'll run away and become a hobo, just like that fellow! I'll run away to the Big Rock Candy Mountains! *(dashes offstage left)*

(GEORGIA PEACH enters from left carrying a placard she mounts on the easel, then addresses audience.)

GEORGIA PEACH: Introducing the World-Famous Weasel Berry Medicine Show and Menagerie, Doctor Mortimer Q. Peach, Proprietor! Coming to your town tonight!

(She curtseys and skips to mid center to stand in front of the scrim; SIX TOWNSFOLK enter in two groups [three from left, three from right] and cross to mid center, each group standing on either side of the scrim, facing each other.)

TOWNSFOLK #1, 2 & 3: It's a medicine show!

TOWNSFOLK #4, 5 & 6: And menagerie!

TOWNSFOLK #1, 2 & 3: Nothing like it in town for months!

TOWNSFOLK #4, 5 & 6: Filled with wonders and merriment!

TOWNSFOLK #1, 2 & 3: Marvelous and fantastic!

TOWNSFOLK #4, 5 & 6: Singular and stupendous!

TOWNSFOLK #1, 2 & 3: Incredible and astonishing!

TOWNSFOLK #4, 5 & 6: Mysterious and bizarre!

(Ben enters from left, studies the placard and moves closer to the crowd at mid center.)

GEORGIA PEACH: Now here he is, the man you've all been waiting for — Doctor Mortimer Q. Peach!

(Townsfolk applaud as DR. MORTIMER Q. PEACH steps out from behind scrim at mid center and stands between the two groups of Townsfolk.)

DR. PEACH: Ladies and gentlemen, fair citizens of the territory! I bid you good evening!

TOWNSFOLK: Good evening, Doctor Peach!

DR. PEACH: Tonight I wish to share with you...the secret of eternal health.

TOWNSFOLK: Eternal health!

DR. PEACH: Are there any among you who would not give your last scrap of earthly treasure to live a long and vigorous life?

(Georgia tugs on Dr. Peach's coat and whispers urgently in his ear.)

DR. PEACH: No! I forbid it! The danger is too great!

GEORGIA PEACH: But, Doctor!

TOWNSFOLK #1: What's the matter with the girl?

DR. PEACH: Never you mind, sir! It is of no concern! *(to Georgia)* Art thou like the adder, deaf! I said no!

GEORGIA PEACH: But, doctor! These people are in danger!

TOWNSFOLK #2: Danger? What's she talking about?

DR. PEACH: I had hoped to spare you goodly citizens the horror—

TOWNSFOLK: Horror!

DR. PEACH: The terror—

TOWNSFOLK: Terror!

DR. PEACH: Of the dreaded Ginthon!

TOWNSFOLK: Ginthon!

DR. PEACH: Why, its very name strikes fear into the heart of every man, woman and child! The Ginthon—

TOWNSFOLK: Ginthon!

DR. PEACH: Is a hideous freak of nature, a monster so base and foul, even its own mother faints at the sight of it!

(SOUND: a whiplash followed by an animal roar and clanking chains comes from behind the scrim. Townsfolk gasp and mumble; Georgia picks up a bucket and goes behind crowd; she smiles and waves at Ben, who smiles and waves back.)

DR. PEACH: *(glances behind him nervously)* Pay no mind, citizens! The creature is fully restrained!

TOWNSFOLK #3: You've got a Ginthon in that tent?

DR. PEACH: Only a small one! But it is a known cannibal. Before it was captured in the jungles of Lamazonia, it daily consumed the flesh of a dozen tender babes washed down with the blood of saintly missionaries.

TOWNSFOLK #4: You've got to let us see it!

DR. PEACH: Oh no, oh no! The horror is too terrible! The terror is too horrible!

GEORGIA PEACH: I'll pay a quarter to see the Ginthon!

TOWNSFOLK #5: Me, too! I'll pay a quarter!

(SOUND: a whiplash followed by an animal roar and clanking chains.)

RUSTY PEACH: *(behind scrim)* Down, down, you beast!

GEORGIA PEACH: I'll pay two quarters!

TOWNSFOLK #6: Me, too!

(Georgia picks up a bucket and goes among Townsfolk collecting money from them, then returns to the front of the scrim.)

DR. PEACH: If you insist! But I must warn you, this creature is among the most repulsive, the most loathsome, the most—

(SOUND: a crescendo of whiplashes, animal roars, clanking chains and loud rips and tears.)

RUSTY PEACH: (behind scrim) Oh my gosh! It's breaking loose from its chains!
TOWNSFOLK: (backing away) It's breaking loose!
DR. PEACH: Do not panic! The creature is restrained!

(Scrim shakes and rattles; sounds continue.)

RUSTY PEACH: (behind scrim) Help! It's, it's, it's choking me!
TOWNSFOLK: It's choking him!
RUSTY PEACH: (behind scrim) Stop, you monster!

(SOUND: firecrackers; scrim shakes more violently; Townsfolk shout in panic.)

GEORGIA PEACH: Run for your lives! The Ginthon is loose!

(As Townsfolk scatter offstage left and right, scrim falls down amidst roars, chain rattling and firecrackers to reveal two brothers, RUSTY PEACH and DUSTY PEACH, standing and laughing at the chaos; Ben remains standing at mid left.)

RUSTY PEACH: (to Dr. Peach) Pop, that was a caution! These yokels are ripe as summer squash!
DUSTY PEACH: (to Georgia) Gee, Sis, you better run for your life! The Ginthon is loose! (laughs)

(Georgia hands money from bucket to Dr. Peach, who pockets it.)

DR. PEACH: Thank you, daughter. That should get 'em warmed up for the big show tomorrow. They'll be spreading the word about us from Tucson to Tucumcari. (yawns) Let's get some shut-eye.

(Dr. Peach exits right; Rusty and Dusty put scrim up again, then exit right; Georgia turns and speaks to Ben; they walk toward each other.)

GEORGIA PEACH: Hello there. Did you enjoy the show?

BEN: What show? There wasn't any Ginthon!

GEORGIA PEACH: There was so!

BEN: Where was it then? I didn't see it!

GEORGIA PEACH: Yes, you did! Do you know what an anagram is?

BEN: An anagram? Of course. It's when you take a word and change the letters around to make another word.

GEORGIA PEACH: Well, change around the letters of Ginthon, and you'll see—

BEN: *(pause, while he calculates)* Nothing! Ginthon is an anagram of Nothing! You cheated those people!

GEORGIA PEACH: We gave them the best thrill of their lives! That's worth fifty cents any day!

BEN: What kind of outfit are you, anyway? I thought you sold patent medicine.

GEORGIA PEACH: We do. That comes the second night. The first night, you have to get the audience excited.

BEN: By scaring them out of their wits?

GEORGIA PEACH: They always come back, and they bring more folks with them. Are you coming back tomorrow?

BEN: I reckon so. I don't have much else to do. You see, I got in a bit of trouble and ran away from home yesterday.

GEORGIA PEACH: I'm sorry. Well, if you want to earn some fast money, you can work with us for a while. We need a good dub.

BEN: A what?

GEORGIA PEACH: I'll explain later. If you need a place to stay, you can share a hotel room with my brothers, Rusty and Dusty. And, oh, where are my manners? My name is Georgia. *(shakes his hand)*

BEN: Georgia? Georgia Peach?

GEORGIA PEACH: My father is Doctor Mortimer Q. Peach. And that's his real name.

BEN: Is he a real doctor?

GEORGIA PEACH: Of course not. He's an actor. One of the best interpreters of Shakespeare who ever trod the boards.

BEN: I'm confused.

GEORGIA PEACH: I'll explain later.

(Rusty and Dusty enter from right and cross to Georgia and Ben.)

RUSTY PEACH: I can't believe those bums!

DUSTY PEACH: Of all the nerve!

GEORGIA PEACH: Ben, these are my brothers, Rusty and Dusty.

RUSTY PEACH: I'm Rusty, and he's Dusty.

DUSTY PEACH: He's Rusty, and I'm hopping mad!

GEORGIA PEACH: What's the matter?

RUSTY PEACH: We went up to our room, and there were two big lunks sleeping in our beds!

DUSTY PEACH: The clerk said they were traveling salesmen and had already booked the room.

RUSTY PEACH: I think they're gunslingers, and the clerk was scared of 'em!

BEN: What are you going to do?

DUSTY PEACH: Give 'em a free show. Come on!

(They cross to mid center and peer at TWO GUNSLINGERS at down right; GUNSLINGER #1 lies on the bench, asleep and snoring, his boots next to the bench; GUNSLINGER #2 is seated to right of bench, wiping his six-shooter with a cloth, his Stetson hat next to him on floor.)

RUSTY PEACH: *(points at Gunslingers)* There they are, the sluga-beds!

DUSTY PEACH: They look powerful mean, don't they?

BEN: *(pulls sling shot from his belt)* The window's open. I bet I can wing him a good one in the noggin.

RUSTY PEACH: Hold on, Wyatt Earp! We don't want to make these pistoleros mad!

DUSTY PEACH: We just want 'em out of our room!

GEORGIA PEACH: I wonder if they've ever seen *Hamlet* ?

RUSTY PEACH: I don't know. But, gee, Ben, you look white as a ghost.

BEN: Huh?

DUSTY PEACH: Put this on. *(reaches into box beside scrim and pulls out a white sheet, which he puts over Ben's head)*

BEN: Hey! What gives!

(Georgia pulls out a container of stage makeup from box and applies white greasepaint and burnt cork to Ben's face.)

BEN: *(squirms)* What the dickens are you doing to my face?

DUSTY PEACH: Quiet! She's making you up as a ghost.

BEN: A ghost?

RUSTY PEACH: He's got me shaking in my boots.

(Georgia finishes applying makeup and straightens Ben's sheet to cover his clothes; Dusty and Rusty push Ben toward the Gunslingers.)

DUSTY PEACH: Ready?

BEN: Ready for what?

RUSTY PEACH: We're going to give these room rustlers a little free entertainment. The ghost scene from Shakepeare's *Hamlet*, as a matter of fact.

GEORGIA PEACH: You step through the window, wave your arms around like you're a dead spirit, and we'll do the rest.

BEN: But I *will* be dead if they catch me!

DUSTY PEACH: Break a leg!

(Dusty pushes Ben forward; Ben stumbles and falls to his knees face to face with Gunslinger #2; Rusty, Dusty and Georgia stand a few feet off, watching and prompting.)

GUNSLINGER #2: *(startled)* What in thunderation?

GEORGIA PEACH: *(moans, ghostlike)* Ohhhhhhh...ooooooh.... *(continues moaning through dialogue)*

RUSTY PEACH: Mark me!

DUSTY PEACH: I will!

RUSTY PEACH: My hour is almost come, when I to sulpherous and tormenting flames must render up myself!

DUSTY PEACH: Alas, poor ghost!

RUSTY PEACH: Alas, poor ghost!

GEORGIA PEACH: Alas, poor ghost who waves his arms so frightfully! *(moans)* Ohhhhhhh...ooooooh....

(Ben waves his arms up and down; Gunslinger #2 points six-shooter at him; Ben waves arms more vigorously.)

GUNSLINGER #2: *(suspiciously)* Who are you?

(Ben waves arms and hobbles around on his knees, evading Gunslinger #2's six-shooter.)

RUSTY PEACH: I am thy father's spirit, doomed for a certain term to walk the night!

DUSTY PEACH: And for the day confined to fast in fires, till the foul crimes done in my days of nature are burnt and purged away!

GUNSLINGER #2: Pa! Is it really you, Pa?

RUSTY PEACH: List, list, o list! If thou didst ever thy dear father love — revenge his foul and most unnatural murder.

GUNSLINGER #2: Murder!?!

DUSTY PEACH: Murder most foul!

GUNSLINGER #2: I didn't mean it, Pa! It were just an accident!

RUSTY PEACH: I could a tale unfold whose lightest word would harrow up they soul!

DUSTY PEACH: Freeze thy young blood!

RUSTY PEACH: Make thy two eyes like stars start from their spheres!

GUNSLINGER #2: *(points at sleeping Gunslinger #1)* It were him, Pa! Him's the one what sunk the axe in your skull and-and-and-and said we should steal the gold for ourselves!

DUSTY PEACH: Thus was I sleeping by a brother's hand — of life, of crown, of queen dispatched!

RUSTY PEACH: O, horrible! O, horrible! Most horrible!

(Gunslinger #2 pulls a saddle bag from under bunch and throws it at Ben's feet.)

GUNSLINGER #2: Here, you take the money, Pa!

GEORGIA PEACH: *(moans)* Ohhhhhhh…ooooooh….

GUNSLINGER #2: And this, too! *(hands his six-shooter to Ben)*

BEN: *(flings six-shooter above his head)* Whaaa!

GUNSLINGER #2: So long, Pa! *(dashes offstage right)*

(Ben stands up, picks up Gunslinger #2's hat and puts it on his head; holding the six-shooter with both hands, he stands over Gunslinger #1, who awakes groggily.)

BEN: Boo!

GUNSLINGER #1: A ghost! And he's killed Buford and took his hat and gun! Whoa, Nellie!

(Gunslinger #1 jumps up, grabs his boots and scurries offstage right; Rusty, Dusty and Georgia come forward and congratulate Ben, who drops six-shooter and takes off sheet.)

RUSTY PEACH: You did it, old socks! You and Bill Shakespeare scared those gunslingers right out of their skins!

DUSTY PEACH: They'll be running till daybreak. Say, what's in the saddle bag?

GEORGIA PEACH: *(kneels and opens bag)* Well, I'll be a flying Dutchman! There's a pound of solid gold coins in here!

BEN: Shouldn't we give it back?

GEORGIA PEACH: Give it back to who? It's stolen!

RUSTY PEACH: Consider it your reward, chum, for helping us get our room back. Georgia, take it to father's room and lock it in his safe.

GEORGIA PEACH: You can spend it when you get to the Big Rock Candy Mountains.

(Georgia exits right; Ben starts to follow her.)

BEN: I sure will. Hey! How did you know—

DUSTY PEACH: Say, old bean, where are you going?

BEN: Ummm, errr, gosh, uhhh...I don't know.

RUSTY PEACH: Sure you do. You're going to join our show.

BEN: But I don't know anything about being in a medicine show!

DUSTY PEACH: You didn't know anything about being a ghost, and look what happened!

RUSTY PEACH: *(puts his arm around Ben's shoulder)* You better stick with us, old toff. You're turning out to be quite a good luck charm!

(LIGHTS OUT FOR TEN SECONDS AS MUSIC UP. MUSIC: "The Garden Where the Praties Grow"; an instrumental introduction, then Rusty enters from behind scrim and sings as LIGHTS COME UP FULL and Townsfolk gather onstage and stand in two groups of three on either side of the scrim, facing each other.)

RUSTY: *(SINGS)*
Have you ever been in love, boys, have you ever felt the pain?
I'd sooner be in jail myself than be in love again!
Though the girl I met was beautiful, I'd have you all to know
That I met her in the garden where the praties grow!

(Dusty enters from behind scrim and sings next verse.)

DUSTY: *(SINGS)*

   I told this pretty colleen I was tired of single life,
   And if she'd no objections, sure, I'd make her my dear wife.
   Says she, "I'll ask my parents and tomorrow let you know,
   If you meet me in the garden where the praties grow!

   (MUSIC ENDS. Rusty and Dusty bow; Townsfolk applaud and cheer. Georgia enters from right and stands at down center, singing to audience as Townsfolk turn to hear her. MUSIC: "Long, Long Ago.")

GEORGIA PEACH: *(SINGS)*

   Tell me the tales that to me were so dear
   Long, long ago — long, long ago
   Sing me the songs I delighted to hear
   Long, long ago...long ago
   Now you are come all my grief is removed
   Let me forget that so long you have roved
   Let me believe that you love as you loved
   Long, long ago...long ago

   (MUSIC ENDS. Townsfolk applaud and cheer; Georgia curtseys and joins Rusty and Dusty at mid center as they sing. MUSIC: "For He's a Jolly Good Fellow.")

RUSTY, DUSTY & GEORGIA: *(SING)*

   For he's a jolly good fellow
   For he's a jolly good fellow
   For he's a jolly good fellow
   Which nobody can deny
   Which nobody can deny
   Which nobody can deny
   For he's a jolly good fellow
   For he's a jolly good fellow
   For he's a jolly good fellow
   Which nobody can deny

   (MUSIC ENDS. Rusty and Dusty bow, Georgia curtseys, Townfolk applaud and cheer.)

TOWNSFOLK #1: Why, this is the best medicine show I've ever seen, bar none!

TOWNSFOLK #2: What kind of medicine are they selling?

TOWNSFOLK #3: Don't know! And don't care, as long as they keep on singing!

GEORGIA PEACH: And now we present one of the most fumigated practitioners of modern science in America today...the inventor, originator and sole prevaricator of the exclusive Weasel Berry Oil Extract...Doctor Mortimer Q. Peach!

(Townsfolk applaud and cheer as Dr. Peach enters from behind scrim; with a curt gesture he quiets them and stands silent for five seconds. Ben enters from right and begins whistling as he saunters across the stage, hands in pockets of his frock coat, derby hat jauntily atop his head; Townsfolk turn and stare at him.)

DR. PEACH: Boy!

(Ben stops at down center and turns half-profile to Dr. Peach.)

BEN: Me?

DR. PEACH: Thy voice is thunder, but thy looks are humble.

BEN: Me?

DR. PEACH: Your humble means match not your haughty spirit!

BEN: Me?

DR. PEACH: Thy world, 'tis full of foul wrongs!

BEN: Me?

TOWNSFOLK: Him?

(Dr. Peach approaches Ben, Townsfolk following behind him.)

DR. PEACH: Earth gapes, hell burns, fiends roar, saints pray! You are malapert!

(Dr. Peach stands next to Ben, Townsfolk surround them in semi-circle.)

DR. PEACH: To the visible eye, this boy appears to be the very apotheosis of health! But, good people, let me assure you — he is a lump of foul deformity, dangerous and unsuspected!

(Dr. Peach turns Ben to face him, then takes careful hold of Ben's right ear and pulls.)

BEN: Ow!
TOWNSFOLK: Gasp!

(Dr. Peach takes careful hold of Ben's left ear and pulls.)

BEN: Ow!
TOWNSFOLK: Gasp!
DR. PEACH: Just as I suspected!

(Dr. Peach reaches under Ben's hat, pulls out a long worm and dangles it in the air for all to see.)

BEN: Ow!
TOWNSFOLK: Gasp!
TOWNSFOLK #4: The boy had a worm in his brain!
TOWNSFOLK #5: It was a foot long!
TOWNSFOLK #6: It was two feet long and had a face like Billy the Kid!
DR. PEACH: *(dangles worm in air)* Out of my sight! Thou dost infect my very eyes! Take with thee my most grievous curse!

(Dr. Peach flings worm into the air above Townsfolk, who shout and scatter, then gather around again in semi-circle as Dr. Peach and Ben face audience.)

DR. PEACH: Do not fear, citizens! This boy suffers in good company. For the latest studies have shown that brain worms can be found to some degree in nearly every human brain!
TOWNSFOLK: Gasp!
DR. PEACH: Even my own!
TOWNSFOLK: Gasp!
DR. PEACH: Even yours!
TOWNSFOLK: Gasp!
DR. PEACH: And yours! *(turns and points to Townsfolk #1)*
TOWNSFOLK: Gasp!
DR. PEACH: And yours! *(points to Townsfolk #2)*
TOWNSFOLK: Gasp!

(Townsfolk #3 faints and is fanned and propped up by oth-

ers; Ben holds right shirt cuff in front of his eyes and reads from it haltingly.)

BEN: Oh, honorable Doctor Peach. Thank you so much for discerning my dreadful malady. How-how-how — oops! *(drops right cuff and lifts up left cuff to read from it)* How can I ever repay you?

DR. PEACH: *(chuckles)* Don't think of repaying me, my brave lad. Why, I wouldn't take one cent for saving your life. I am a scientist!

(Dr. Peach bows; Townsfolk applaud.)

DR. PEACH: However, kindly ask yourself this question: what is the price you would be willing to pay...to be forever free from the worm of conscience begnawing thy soul?

BEN: Ummm, errr, gosh, uhhh...*(reads right cuff)* I'd pay one whole dollar for a bottle of Dr. Peach's Patented Weasel Berry Oil Extract!

(Dr. Peach bows; Townsfolk applaud; Georgia runs up to Dr. Peach with a medicine bottle.)

DR. PEACH: This remarkable potion is made from the most potent mineral extracts found in a secret mountain spring outside Palenville, New York, the home town of that modern Methusaleh, Rip Van Winkle himself. Where his grandson, Henry Van Winkle, has a special garden of herbs and berries which he himself tends. Did I say the grandson of Rip Van Winkle? Yes, I believe I did, and he is one hundred and two years of age — a good fifteen years older than his own father — as hale and hearty as a man of twenty-five!

BEN: Even though he's a hundred and two!

DR. PEACH: And getting younger each and every day! Now, I have but a few small samples of this marvelous elixir still in stock—

(Rusty brings a case of medicine bottles to down center, Dusty collects money in bucket as Townsfolk surge forward to buy bottles.)

TOWNSFOLK #4: I'll take two!

TOWNSFOLK #5: I'll take five!

TOWNSFOLK #6: I'll take a dozen! And one for my old mule, Sam! He's already outlived my first three husbands!

(Rusty and Dusty move offstage left, Townsfolk clamoring and following behind them.)

DR. PEACH: Don't crush! There's plenty more in the wagon! *(to Georgia)* Daughter, saddle up the horses; we'll be off soon as the boys return. *(to Ben)* Good sir, for the supply and profit of our hope, your visitation shall receive such thanks as fits a king's remembrance. *(exits left)*

BEN: What did he say?

GEORGIA PEACH: He said you were a good dub, and he hopes you'll work with us again in the next town.

BEN: Gosh, Georgia, I don't know. I mean, what's in that old medicine stuff, anyway? Smells like baked beans and turpentine to me!

GEORGIA PEACH: With a few drops of soapweed, ginseng and cottonseed oil mixed in. It's perfectly harmless — even to mules and horses.

BEN: You're all a bunch of actors! You don't believe a word you say to those people!

GEORGIA PEACH: And what do *you* believe in, Ben? *(sings "The Big Rock Candy Mountains")*
O, the birds and the bees and the peppermint trees,
The fudge cake springs where the whang doodle sings
In the Big Rock Candy Mountains.

BEN: *You! You* were the hungry hobo!

GEORGIA PEACH: I really *was* hungry, too. I'm sorry if I put you in trouble with your Aunt. But I thought you might have more fun if you got away from home for a little while. *(takes out harmonica from her dress pocket)* Do you want to play my harmonica? *(toots harmonica)*

(Aunt Beatrice enters from right and sees Ben.)

AUNT BEATRICE: Benjamin! My lands, what are you doing in that outlandish get-up!?!

BEN: I'm being a dub, Aunt Beatrice.

AUNT BEATRICE: Of all the confounded nonsense! You give that costume back and come home this very instant! Supper's waiting, and I'm not cooking it twice! *(exits right)*

GEORGIA PEACH: You better go home, Ben. There really are no Big Rock Candy Mountains.

BEN: It's just make-believe?

GEORGIA PEACH: Sometimes people want to believe in things they know can't possibly be true.

BEN: Like brain worms and ginthons?

GEORGIA PEACH: *Especially* brain worms and ginthons! *(laughs)*

BEN: Well, then I reckon I'll keep on believing in the Big Rock Candy Mountains.

(MUSIC: "The Big Rock Candy Mountains"; Entire Cast enters and joins on final chorus.)

BEN: *(SINGS)*
In the Big Rock Candy Mountains
There's a land that's fair and bright,

GEORGIA PEACH: *(SINGS)*
Where the handouts grow on bushes,
And you sleep out every night.

BEN & GEORGIA PEACH: *(SING)*
Where the boxcars all are empty,
And the sun shines every day.

ENTIRE CAST: *(SING)*
O, the birds and the bees and the peppermint trees,
The fudge cake springs where the whang doodle sings,
Where there ain't no snow and the wind don't blow,
Where they boiled in oil the inventor of toil,
There's a lake of stew and chocolate, too,
In the Big Rock Candy Mountains.

(LIGHTS OUT.)

THE END

The Big Rock Candy Mountains
(traditional, arranged by L.E. McCullough)

The Garden Where the Praties Grow
(words & music: Johnny Patterson, arr. by L.E. McCullough)

Have you ev- er been in love, boys, have you ev- er felt the pain? I'd soon- er be in jail my- self than be in love a- gain! Though the girl I met was beau- ti- ful, I'd have you all to know, that I met her in the gar- den where the pra- ties grow!

Long, Long Ago
(words & music by Thomas Bayly, arr. by L.E. McCullough)

Tell me the tales that to me were so dear; long, long a- go, long, long a- go; Sing me the songs I de- ligh- ted to hear; long, long a- go... long a- go Now you are come all my grief is re- moved; Let me for- get that so long you have roved; Let me be- lieve that you love as you loved; long, long a- go... long a- go

For He's a Jolly Good Fellow
(traditional, arranged by L.E. McCullough)

For he's a jol- ly good fel- low; For he's a jol- ly good

fel- low; For he's a jol- ly good fel- low which no- bo- dy can de-

ny Which no- bo- dy can de- ny; Which no- bo- dy can de-

ny; For he's a jol- ly good fel- low; For he's a jol- ly good

fel- low; For he's a jol- ly good fel- low which no- bo- dy can de- ny

"HAVE FLOSS, WILL TRAVEL":

THE EVER-SO-TRUE SAGA OF HIRAM T. McROOT, FRONTIER DENTIST

Many towns in the West sprouted up literally overnight as a railroad depot was established, a gold or silver mine was opened or cattle drives began coming to town. Such instant prosperity attracted criminals; a few towns such as Dodge City, Kansas, Tombstone, Arizona, Abilene, Texas and Deadwood, South Dakota achieved national reputations for extreme lawlessness that featured frequent public shootouts between rival gunfighters. After two or three years, however, the stable elements of a town — merchants, church leaders, craftsmen and teachers — usually succeeded in expelling the troublemakers and establishing law and order. In some cases, former gunslingers were brought in to control the bad elements, on the theory that there was no honor among thieves and a sheriff with a criminal background would have the upper hand in dealing with outlaws.

TIME: Summer, 1878

PLACE: Buzzard Belch, Colorado

RUNNING TIME: 25 minutes

CAST: 13 actors, min. 6 boys, 1 girl

Hiram T. McRoot, D.D.S.	Mayor Buncum
Miss Savannah, a Saloon Keeper	2 Gunslingers
Scribbles O'Shea, a Newspaperman	Telegraph Operator
Hog-Eye Hogan, an Outlaw	3 Townsfolk
Pottem Porter, an Undertaker	Pluggem Porter, an Undertaker

STAGE SET: At down right is a table and chair; at mid center is a hitching rail and a sign hanging over it reading "Buzzard Belch, Col. — Pop. 222"; at down left is a sign hanging that reads "Boot Hill ➔ "

PROPS: towel, notebook, pencil, 4 pistols, telegraph key, 2 marker pens, newspaper, small black bag, handkerchief, pliers, putty knife, bowl, small hand mirror, business card, large cardboard tooth

EFFECTS: Sound — gun shots

MUSIC: *Billy Boy, Camptown Races, Tenting Tonight, Miles of Smiles*

COSTUMES: Characters dress in standard Western costume; Pottem and Pluggem Porter wear black undertaker outfits; Hog-Eye Hogan wears an eye-patch over one eye; Miss Savannah Jane can have a plumed headdress; Scribbles O'Shea can wear an eye-shade visor; Hiram T. McRoot wears a period dark dress suit and, if desired, a white modern dentist's smock underneath

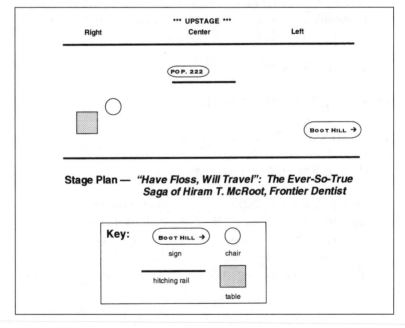

Stage Plan — *"Have Floss, Will Travel"*: The Ever-So-True Saga of Hiram T. McRoot, Frontier Dentist

(LIGHTS UP FULL on the main street of Buzzard Belch. At down left stands SCRIBBLES O'SHEA, writing in a notebook. At mid center is a hitching rail; TWO GUNSLINGERS lounge against it. At down right is a table and chair; MISS SAVANNAH JANE, a saloon keeper, has one foot on the chair and idly polishes the table top with a towel as she sings off-key. MUSIC: "Billy Boy.")

MISS SAVANNAH JANE: *(SINGS)*
Where have you been, Billy Boy, Billy Boy?
Where have you been, charming Billy?
I have been down the lane to see Savannah Jane;
She's a young thing and cannot leave her mammy.

SCRIBBLES O'SHEA: *(to audience)* Oh, hello there! Welcome to a typical morning in Buzzard Belch, Colorado. My name is O'Shea — Scribbles O'Shea, they call me. I'm the editor of the town newspaper, the Buzzard Belch Bugle. That warbling songbird you heard piercing the mountain air is Miss Savannah Jane. She runs the town saloon and keeps everybody in a friendly frame of mind.

(GUNSLINGER #1 gives GUNSLINGER #2 a push in the shoulder.)

GUNSLINGER #1: Oh, yeh! Well, I say it is!
GUNSLINGER #2: And I say it isn't!

(Gunslingers draw pistols and shoot; Gunslinger #1 falls to ground dead as Gunslinger #2 blows smoke from his pistol and re-holsters it. SOUND: gun shots.)

MISS SAVANNAH JANE: *(shouts, without turning to look)* Man for breakfast!

(POTTEM PORTER and PLUGGEM PORTER, two undertakers, march out from left and lift up Gunslinger #1, displaying him to audience and singing. MUSIC: "Billy Boy.")

POTTEM & PLUGGEM PORTER: *(SING)*
Oh, you have been killed very dead, very dead;
You have been killed most completely.
Since you didn't leave a will, you'll be buried in Boot Hill
With the others who had itchy trigger fingers.

(Pluggem Porter takes a marker pen and crosses out "222" on sign, replacing it with "221"; Pottem and Pluggem carry off Gunslinger #1 left.)

SCRIBBLES O'SHEA: Like I said, just a typical morning in Buzzard Belch. Oh, those fellows in the black suits? They're the Porter Brothers, Pottem and Pluggem. They run the mortuary, and they keep plenty busy. Why, it seems like the cemetery has more people in it than the town! And this has become greatly distressing to the honest citizens of Buzzard Belch.

(THREE TOWNSFOLK enter from right, stop to the left of O'Shea and sing to each other. MUSIC: "Camptown Races.")

TOWNFOLK #1: *(SINGS)*
Buzzard Belch is a big disgrace—
TOWNSFOLK #2 & 3: *(SING)*
Doo-dah, doo-dah!
TOWNFOLK #1: *(SINGS)*
Outlaws shooting all over the place—
TOWNSFOLK #2 & 3: *(SING)*
All the doo-dah day!
TOWNFOLK #1: *(SINGS)*
What hero can be found
To tame this wild town?
TOWNSFOLK #2 & 3: *(SING)*
Somebody's got to get on the stick
And settle this doo-dah quick!

(Gunslinger #2 shoots pistol in air. SOUND: two quick gun shots punctuating the end of the song.)

GUNSLINGER #2: Eeeee-hah!

(MAYOR BUNCUM enters from right, smiles and tips hat to Miss Savannah Jane, who turns her head away without smiling; Mayor Buncum crosses to center where he is met by Townsfolk #1, 2 & 3 who circle him.)

TOWNFOLK #1: Mayor Buncum!
TOWNFOLK #2: Mayor Buncum!
TOWNFOLK #3: Mayor Buncum!

MAYOR BUNCUM: That's my name, don't wear it out!

TOWNFOLK #1: You're the mayor!

TOWNFOLK #2: You're the mayor!

TOWNFOLK #3: You're the mayor!

MAYOR BUNCUM: Yes, I know; what's all the shout?

TOWNFOLK #1: As citizens of Buzzard Belch—

TOWNFOLK #2: We're asking you to put a squelch—

TOWNFOLK #3: To the mayhem and slaughter—

TOWNFOLK #1: That frightens our daughters—

TOWNFOLK #2: And keeps our fair city—

TOWNFOLK #3: A hostage to banditti!

MAYOR BUNCUM: And just what am I to do?

TOWNFOLK #1: Get a marshal!

TOWNFOLK #2: Get a sheriff!

TOWNFOLK #3: Get a ranger!

MISS SAVANNAH JANE: Get a clue!
   The last five marshals we've had
   Were laid down in the dust.
   There's not a lawman alive
   Would risk his neck for the likes of us!

   (Miss Savannah Jane sings. MUSIC: "Billy Boy.")

MISS SAVANNAH JANE: *(SINGS)*
   Cause we're a bad little town, little town, little town;
   We're a bad little town and awful dirty.
MAYOR BUNCUM: *(SINGS)*
   We've got cheats and desperados and rustlers on the tear;
TOWNSFOLK #1, 2 & 3: *(SING)*
   Why can't we find an honest man somewhere?

   (TELEGRAPH OPERATOR enters from right with telegraph key and sits at table, tapping out a message.)

SCRIBBLES O'SHEA: Down at the telegraph office, a last frantic message was sent to the Governor.

   (Telegraph Operator sings. MUSIC: "Camptown Races.")

TELEGRAPH OPERATOR: *(SINGS)*
   S-O-S, this is our cry!
   Doo-dah, doo-dah!

Help us now before we die!
All the doo-dah day!

TOWNSFOLK, MAYOR & MISS SAVANNAH JANE: *(SING)*
Listen to our plea!
End this misery!
Whoever hears this S-O-S,
We're in a terrible mess!

(SOUND: two quick gun shots punctuating the end of the song. Telegraph Operator slumps over onto table, dead; Pottem and Pluggem Porter enter from left, carry Telegraph Operator offstage right; Gunslinger #2 takes a pen and crosses out "221" on sign, replacing it with "220." LIGHTS OUT BRIEFLY, THEN UP FULL. At down right Miss Savannah Jane has one foot on the chair and idly polishes the table top with a towel; standing at down left is Scribbles O'Shea, flourishing a newspaper.)

SCRIBBLES O'SHEA: Extra, extra! Read all about it! The Governor has promised to send assistance! Citizens of Buzzard Belch eagerly await the next stage from Denver!

(Mayor and Townsfolk #1, 2 & 3 march in from left and stand at mid center in front of hitching rail; Pottem & Pluggem Porter march in and stand at down right to the right of Miss Savannah Jane. MUSIC: "Tenting Tonight.")

TOWNSFOLK & MAYOR: *(SING)*
We are waiting tonight for the Denver stage,
Hoping relief is near.
A marshal, a sheriff, an Indian brave—
A man who knows no fear.

MISS SAVANNAH JANE: *(SINGS)*
Many are the hearts that are weary tonight,
Wondering who has answered the call.

POTTEM & PLUGGEM PORTER: *(SING)*
Many are the eyes that are greedy tonight,
Waiting for the shovel to fall.

ALL: *(SING)*
Waiting tonight, waiting tonight,
Waiting for the Denver stage.

(SOUND: a gun shot offstage. HOG-EYE HOGAN enters from left with pistol drawn, scowls at O'Shea, and taps newspaper with pistol.)

TOWNSFOLK & MAYOR: It's Hog-Eye Hogan!

HOG-EYE HOGAN: Does this here newsrag say anything about me — Hog-Eye Hogan, worstest outlaw in all of Buzzard Belch and therefore all of Colorado and possibly even the whole United States?

SCRIBBLES O'SHEA: *(gives newspaper to Hogan)* G-g-g-go ahead and read for yourself, M-m-m-mister Hog-Eye.

HOG-EYE HOGAN: You know I can't read!

SCRIBBLES O'SHEA: T-t-t-that's true, but you s-s-s-sure can s-s-s-shoot people!

HOG-EYE HOGAN: Darn tootin'! I aim to shoot this Stranger afore he has time to jingle his spurs. And then I'm gonna marry Miss Savannah Jane!

TOWNSFOLK & MAYOR: Marry Savannah Jane!

HOG-EYE HOGAN:
Oh, we'll have the nicest wedding
Buzzard Belch has ever seen!
Then I'll whisk her to my hideout,
And she'll be my outlaw queen.

MISS SAVANNAH JANE: Hah!
I'll ne'er consent to be your bride,
You poor deluded soul!
Even if you filled me with
A hundred bullet holes!

SCRIBBLES O'SHEA: *(points out at audience)* Here comes the stage!

TOWNSFOLK & MAYOR: *(pointing at audience)* The stage! The stage!

(All characters gather lengthwise in two rows at down center and stare out at audience, the first row kneeling/crouching, the second row leaning over them.)

FIRST ROW: That him? That him?

SECOND ROW: Can't tell! Can't tell!

(HIRAM T. McROOT, carrying a small black bag, enters from

left — behind the other characters, who do not see him. At mid center, he loudly clears his throat.)

HIRAM T. McROOT: Ahem!

(All characters whirl around and divide into two groups on either side of McRoot.)

ALL CHARACTERS: It's him!

HIRAM T. McROOT: *(pauses)* Evening, folks. I take it this is Buzzard Belch?

(No one replies; McRoot begins strolling around the stage, as the other characters follow him at a distance; Scribbles O'Shea stands at down left and addresses audience; Gunslingers #1 and 2 enter from right and carry table and chair to down center.)

SCRIBBLES O'SHEA:
Well, the Stranger commenced to rambling
Up and down the street.
He visited the restaurant
Where he had a bite to eat.

He checked in at the clothier's
And bought a new hat brim.
Then went on to the barber
And got his whiskers trimmed.

And everyone was wondering
About who he just might be.
Perhaps he was a Pinkerton?
Or a Secret Service deputy?

Or maybe a bounty hunter
Armed with warrants for arrest?
Could be an Army officer
Itching for a test?

Or maybe a bold assassin
With a past as black as coal,
And a laundry list of dirty deeds
Etched upon his wicked soul?

(McRoot stops at down left; he draws out a small sign from his bag and hangs it over the Boot Hill sign.)

SCRIBBLES O'SHEA:
  But suddenly the Stranger stopped
  Next to the undertaker store,
  And produced a wooden shingle
  That he hung upon the door.
HIRAM T. McROOT: Hiram T. McRoot, D.D.S.
ALL CHARACTERS: A dentist!?!
MAYOR: We sent an SOS for a DDS!
MISS SAVANNAH JANE:
  Well, let me tell you cowards,
  And I'll say it loud and clear;
  He's the only man who's man enough
  To stick his nose in here!
HOG-EYE HOGAN: *(to McRoot)*
  Now, listen to me, pardner,
  And listen to me true;
  This town ain't nowhere big enough
  For the likes of me and you.

  I challenge you to a gun fight,
  So choose your weapons free;
  And, folks, you better get indoors
  To watch this shootin' jamboree!

(Everyone backs away from McRoot and Hogan; McRoot takes a handkerchief from his bag and holds it well in front of him.)

HIRAM T. McROOT: Good sir, would you mind holding this handkerchief?
HOG-EYE HOGAN: *(reluctantly takes the handkerchief)* What is this? A dang souvenir? *(laughs, sniffs handkerchief)* Haw-haw-haw! I'm gonna fill him full of lead, and he's givin' me a souvenir! *(takes a big sniff, laughs)* Haw-haw-haw! *(swoons and falls to ground)*
HIRAM T. McROOT: A souvenir, yes, indeed. An ether-filled souvenir of your first trip to the dentist!
POTTEM PORTER: Is he dead?

PLUGGEM PORTER: Can we bury him?

HIRAM T. McROOT: He's not dead! He's merely anesthetized! Get him in that chair!

(Pottem and Pluggem Porter carry Hogan to the chair and turn the chair around so Hogan faces away from audience; McRoot turns to Miss Savannah Jane.)

HIRAM T. McROOT: Nurse, please set my bag on the operating table.

(Miss Savannah Jane picks up bag and follows McRoot to the table.)

HIRAM T. McROOT: And prepare for major oral surgery!

ALL CHARACTERS: Gasp!

(Characters stand behind McRoot and Miss Savannah Jane to watch the operation, grimacing as it progresses. McRoot snaps his fingers and Miss Savannah Jane hands him a pliers and putty knife, which he shows the crowd; Miss Savannah Jane pulls a small bowl out of the bag and holds it. From audience's viewpoint, it should look as if McRoot is digging and pulling items out of Hogan's mouth and tossing them into the bowl.)

SCRIBBLES O'SHEA:
Well, that tooth jockey was some punkins!
He cleaned the outlaw's pearlies
And scraped off yards of plaque.
He gussied up the front teeth
Then started on the back.

Oh, you'd not believe the things were found
Between that bandit's grimy lips;
Bits of grass and bark and straw
And pins and paper clips.

There were collard greens and flapjack crumbs,
Pure piles of apple cores;
A shoelace eye and a fresh corn ear,
The brass knob from a kitchen door.

A canary bird and a saddle ring
Two shoes that did not match;

A cooking spoon, a deck of cards
And a broken window latch.

Buried deep in that mouth of grit
All caked with mud and rust,
Were coffee cups and branding irons
And about four pounds of dust.

Stirrup strings and chicken bones
Were the last to come unloosed,
Behind a flood of melon seeds
And the feathers of a goose.

(McRoot stops extracting and takes a step back to smile at his handiwork.)

HIRAM T. McROOT: Nurse, please hand the patient a mirror!

(Miss Savannah Jane takes a mirror out of the bag and hands it to Hogan, who turns around in the chair and gazes at his mouth in the mirror; McRoot sings to Hogan. MUSIC: "Billy Boy.")

HIRAM T. McROOT: *(SINGS)*
Now your teeth are clean, Hog-Eye Hogan.
Now your teeth are clean, charming Hog-Eye.
So be of goodly cheer, you can smile without fear;
You're no longer gross and slimy.
HOG-EYE HOGAN: *(SINGS)*
I feel so minty fresh, yes I do, yes I do.
I feel so minty fresh and so charming.
HIRAM T. McROOT: *(SINGS)*
Brush between each snack; in six months again come back,
And we'll fit you with a lovely set of dentures.
HIRAM T. McROOT: That will be one dollar, please! Next patient!

(Hogan gets up from chair; Gunslinger #1 hops into chair and opens his mouth wide.)

GUNSLINGER #1: Aaaahhhh!

(McRoot mimes working in Gunslinger #1's mouth as Miss Savannah Jane packs pliers, putty knife, bowl and mirror into bag; other characters stand and admire each other's teeth.)

SCRIBBLES O'SHEA: That drill-slinger was the fastest draw with a forceps I ever did see! He took on every outlaw in Buzzard Belch and cleaned up the town in no time. Within a week, there wasn't a sore pair of gums or a pistol-packing hombre to be seen in the whole entire county!

(McRoot takes bag from Miss Savannah Jane.)

HIRAM T. McROOT: Citizens, my work here is done. Reckon I'll be movin' on up the trail.

MISS SAVANNAH JANE: But you can't leave, darling! You have won my tender heart and convinced me to give up my scandalous ways!

HIRAM T. McROOT: Ma'am, you and I both know that's just the flouride talking. The life of a dentist-for-hire is no life for a lady. *(kisses her hand)* I bid you all adieu! *(exits left)*

SCRIBBLES O'SHEA: And that was the last we ever saw of the mysterious Stranger who cleaned up Buzzard Belch!

MAYOR BUNCUM: Look! He left this card! *(holds up business card)*

MISS SAVANNAH JANE: *(reads card)* "Have floss, will travel!" *(clasps hands together)* My hero!

(Entire Cast except McRoot gather at center stage and sing. MUSIC: "Miles of Smiles.")

ENTIRE CAST: *(SING)*
> Now that is the story of a dentist
> Who rode through the West long ago;
> He fought against cavities and outlaws
> Wherever abscesses did grow.

(McRoot enters waving his hat and brandishing, as if it were a six-shooter, a pliers holding a large cardboard tooth.)

ENTIRE CAST: *(SING)*
> Doctor McRoot, the frontier dentist,
> He saved us from plaque and decay;
> His extractions brought satisfaction

And plenty of smiles our way…
And plenty of smiles our way…
Yes, plenty of smiles,
For miles and miles,
Yes, plenty of smiles our way.

(LIGHTS OUT.)

THE END

Tenting Tonight
(music: Walter Kittredge, words: L.E. McCullough)

We are wait- ing to- night for the Den-ver stage, hop- ing re- lief is near. A mar-shal, a she- riff, an In- di- an brave — a man who knows no fear. Ma-ny are the hearts that are wea-ry to-night, wond-ering who has an- swered call. Ma-ny are the eyes that are gree-dy to-night, wait-ing for the sho- vel to fall. Wait- ing to- night, wait- ing to- night, wait-ing for the Den- ver stage.

words © L.E. McCullough 1997

Camptown Races
(music: Stephen Foster, words: L.E. McCullough)

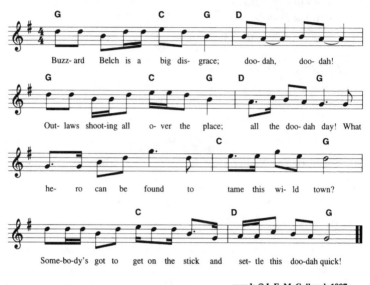

Buzz- ard Belch is a big dis- grace; doo- dah, doo- dah!

Out- laws shoot-ing all o- ver the place; all the doo- dah day! What

he- ro can be found to tame this wi- ld town?

Some-bo-dy's got to get on the stick and set- tle this doo-dah quick!

Billy Boy
(music: traditional, words: L.E. McCullough)

Where have you been, Bil- ly Boy, Bil- ly Boy?

Where have you been, char- ming Bil- ly? I have

been down the lane to see Sa- van- nah Jane; she's a

young thing and can- not leave her mam- my.

Miles of Smiles

(words & music by L.E. McCullough)

Now that is the sto-ry of a den-tist Who rode through the West long a-go; He fought a-gainst ca-vi-ties and bold out-laws, Wher-e-ver ab-scess-es did grow. Doc-tor Mc-Root, the fron-tier den-tist, Yes, he saved us from plaque and de-cay; His ex-trac-tions brought sat-is-fac-tion And plen-ty of smi-les our way... And plen-ty of smi-les our way... Yes, plen-ty of smi-les, for mi-les and mi-les, Yes plen-ty of smi-les our wa-ay.

© L.E. McCullough 1997

JESSE JAMES: BLOOD ON THE SADDLE

The terrible mass killing and destruction of the Civil War did not create the Western outlaw, but it certainly helped foster the unsettled social climate that gave opportunity and refuge to bandits and lawbreakers roaming the American West. As more and more settlers moved into the West, conflicts arose among homesteaders, cattle ranchers, sheep herders and miners; these conflicts were all too frequently settled by violence. The media of the time — newspapers, crime magazines and adventure novels — glamorized outlaws like Sam Bass and Billy the Kid, whose callous crimes were often portrayed sympathetically as strikes against government and business repression. The exploits of Missouri bandit Jesse James, in particular, spawned much folklore; even as late as the 1940s, several men claimed to be "the real" Jesse James.

TIME: January 22, 1929

PLACE: A bus station, St. Joseph, Missouri

RUNNING TIME: 25 minutes

CAST: 33 actors, min. 15 boys, 3 girls

Freddie	Mabel
Harv	Elmer
Jesse James as Child	Martha Ann
Jesse James as Adult	School Bully
Frank James	William Quantrill
6 Lawrence Citizens	Zerelda Mims (Mrs. Jesse James)
Cole Younger	Bob Younger
Liberty Bank Teller	Liberty Bystander
2 Reporters	Northfield Bank Teller
3 Northfield Citizens	Northfield Bank Customer
Bill Chadwell	Clell Miller
D.L. Bligh	Robert Ford
Charlie Ford	

STAGE SET: podium and bench at down right; sign reading "Bus Depot, St. Joseph, Mo." hanging mid right; table and 2 chairs at down left

PROPS: newspaper, broom, nail file, megaphone, college pennant, apple, cake, 3 rifles, 4 pistols, saber, dollar bills, 2 pencils, 2 notepads, bag of coins, deck of cards, handkerchief, silver dollar

EFFECTS: Sound — thundering horses; gun shots

MUSIC: *Jesse James*

COSTUMES: Freddie dresses as a 1929 college student with a sweater and perhaps a sporty cap; Mabel wears a simple floral dress; Harv wears a dark suit with a bow tie; Elmer wears janitor overalls; during the Civil War scene William Quantrill, Frank James, Cole Younger and Jesse James wear a military-style grey jacket or Confederate cap; other 19th-century characters wear standard garb according to age and occupation; during outlaw scenes, Jesse James, Frank James, Cole Younger, Bob Younger, Bill Chadwell and Clell Miller wear white shirts, dark vests, colored bandanas and wide-brimmed Western hats; bank tellers wear eye-shade visors

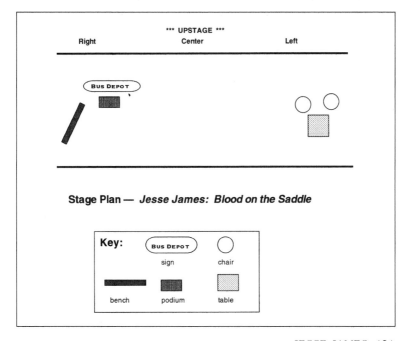

Stage Plan — *Jesse James: Blood on the Saddle*

(LIGHTS UP FULL on the interior of a bus station in St. Joseph, Missouri. At down right HARV, a middle-aged man, sits on a bench reading a newspaper next to a young college student, FREDDIE, who idly twirls a pennant with "U. M." on it. The ticket seller, MABEL, stands behind a podium, filing her nails. The elderly janitor, ELMER, sweeps the floor at down left, moving slowly toward center and whistling the melody of an old folk tune, "Jesse James." Mabel picks up a megaphone and shouts into it.)

MABEL: The ten o'clock bus for Kansas City, St. Louis and points east has been delayed. All passengers are advised to stand by for further details.

FREDDIE: Oh no! My final history exam is tomorrow morning! I have to be back at college tonight!

HARV: Don't get your tail feathers all flung up, sonny. Here, read about President Hoover's latest brainstorm on Prohibition. *That'll* be history in a few years.

FREDDIE: Thanks.

(Freddie takes the front part of newspaper, leafs through it and suddenly peers intently at an article.)

FREDDIE: Gosh, look at this! Wyatt Earp died last week! Age eighty, from natural causes, in Los Angeles.

HARV: Who?

FREDDIE: Wyatt Earp, the famous gunslinger and frontier marshal. Don't you remember? The Shootout at the O.K. Corral? Tombstone? Dodge City?

HARV: Oh, yeh. All that Wild West stuff.

FREDDIE: *(rapturously)* The Wild West! I wonder what it was really like when there were gunslingers and lawmen dueling in the streets? Wyatt Earp, Billy the Kid, Jesse James — guess they're all gone now.

MABEL: I wouldn't be too sure.

FREDDIE: What do you mean?

MABEL: Jesse James for instance.

FREDDIE: Jesse James the bank robber?

HARV: He wasn't any Sunday School preacher.

FREDDIE: Begging your pardon, ma'am, but Jesse James was killed almost fifty years ago — right here in St. Joseph! I read about it in our history book.

HARV: Books don't always tell the whole story, sonny.

MABEL: Don't tell the whole story at all.

FREDDIE: Then, what *is* the whole story? Are you saying Jesse James is still alive?

(Elmer chuckles; Mabel, Harv and Freddie turn sharply and look at Elmer at down center, who stops chuckling, then turns to look sheepishly for a moment at Mabel, Harv and Freddie before starting to sweep again.)

HARV: Well now, the whole story is a long story. And it starts a-way back in 1847, when Jesse Woodson James was born in Clay County, Missouri, near the town of Kearney...

(LIGHTS OUT; MUSIC: "Jesse James" sung offstage.)

SINGER: *(SINGS)*
You've heard of bandits brave in all their glory
In history you've often read their names
But lend an ear and you will hear the story
About that famous bandit Jesse James

Jesse left a wife to mourn for his life
Three children, sad and brave
But the dirty little coward that shot Mr. Howard
Has laid Jesse James in his grave

(LIGHTS UP CENTER AND LEFT; JESSE JAMES AS A CHILD kneels at down center, eating an apple.)

HARV: *(o.s.)* Jesse's pa was a Baptist missionary, who died of pneumonia searching for gold in California when Jesse was only three, and his older brother, Frank, was just seven. The James boys and their two younger sisters grew up poor but honest. Jesse, in particular, was known as a protector of younger, weaker children.

(MARTHA ANN enters from left, sobbing.)

YOUNG JESSE JAMES: Say, Martha Ann, what are you crying about?

MARTHA ANN: That bully stole my lunch!

(She points to SCHOOL BULLY who strolls in from right, gobbling a piece of cake.)

SCHOOL BULLY: Mmm-mmm-good! This cake is right tasty!

(Jesse rises and confronts School Bully.)

YOUNG JESSE JAMES: Say there! Did you take Martha Ann's lunch?
SCHOOL BULLY: So what if I did, squirt? Want it back?

(School Bully opens his food-filled mouth and mockingly sticks out his tongue; Jesse socks him in the stomach and wrestles him to the ground, quickly pinning him.)

SCHOOL BULLY: *(squealing)* Help! Help! Uncle! Uncle!
YOUNG JESSE JAMES: You apologize to Martha Ann!
SCHOOL BULLY: All right, all right! *(sniffs, whimpers)* I'm s-s-s-sorry.
YOUNG JESSE JAMES: *(throttles School Bully)* Sorry, what?
SCHOOL BULLY: S-s-s-sorry for stealing your lunch.
YOUNG JESSE JAMES: *(throttles School Bully)* And?
SCHOOL BULLY: And...and...and I won't do it again!

(Jesse releases the School Bully who runs offstage right; Jesse dusts his hands, tips his hat to Martha Ann and exits left, followed by a grateful Martha Ann.)

MABEL: *(o.s.)* But Jesse's carefree childhood ended with the coming of the War Between the States — the American Civil War. In this terrible conflict which set brother fighting against brother, Missouri and Kansas were called "border states"; neither were officially on the Union or the Confederate side. However, armed gangs sympathetic to the anti-slavery North — called "jayhawkers" — and the pro-slavery South — called "bushwhackers" — roamed the countryside, stealing and killing in the name of patriotism.

(WILLIAM QUANTRILL [brandishing a saber], FRANK JAMES [brandishing a rifle] and COLE YOUNGER [brandishing a pistol] march in from left; Frank James and Cole Younger fall in behind Quantrill at down center. MUSIC: "Jesse James" sung offstage.)

SINGER *(SINGS)*

> When Jesse was a lad, he joined the bad guerillas
> And there he learned to play their wicked games
> With brother Frank and other famous killers
> Began the bold career of Jesse James

MABEL: *(o.s.)* In 1861, Frank James joined a bushwhacker band led by William Quantrill, one of the bloodiest guerilla leaders of the war. Frank and Cole Younger, a neighbor from a slave-owning family down the road from the James home, took part in several massacres by Quantrill, including the burning of Lawrence, Kansas on August 21, 1863.

(SIX LAWRENCE CITIZENS enter from left, see William Quantrill, Frank James and Cole Younger and cower; actors mime action during ensuing dialogue. SOUND: thundering horses, gun shots, screams.)

HARV: *(o.s.)* Quantrill gave orders to kill every single man and boy in Lawrence — and 185 men and boys were slaughtered as their wives, mothers, sisters and daughters wept and pleaded for mercy. The entire town was burned to the ground, and Quantrill's Raiders fled into the Kansas night.

(Lawrence Citizens die and are dragged offstage left by Quantrill, Frank James and Younger. ADULT JESSE JAMES enters from right, marching to down center and standing at attention with his pistol held in front of him.)

HARV: *(o.s.)* There is no evidence that Jesse James took part in the burning of Lawrence. But he was already a deft hand at killing. At sixteen he joined a bushwhacker group led by one of Quantrill's lieutenants, Bloody Bill Anderson — a thoroughly intolerant man who tied his victims' scalps to his saddle as trophies.

(Jesse mimes shooting in a battle, crouching and firing at stage left.)

HARV: *(o.s.)* Jesse fought several battles against Union sympathizers with Anderson and Quantrill until in August, 1864 at Flat Rock Ford, a rifle bullet caught him in the lung.

(SOUND: gun shot; Jesse falls, rises slowly and begins limping offstage left; ZERELDA MIMS enters from left and helps Jesse offstage left.)

HARV: *(o.s.)* He survived this wound and rode with Anderson again, taking part in a horrendous massacre of civilians and Union prisoners at Centralia, Missouri, where he was shot in the left side and arm. And again, a few weeks after the Civil War had officially ended, Jesse received another bullet in the lung during a final skirmish with Union troops. His cousin, Zerelda Mims, took Jesse home and nursed him back to health. They fell in love and were married a few years later.

(LIBERTY BANK TELLER enters from left and sits on chair behind table at down left, counting dollar bills.)

MABEL: *(o.s.)* After the Civil War ended, many ex-soldiers continued to fight their own private wars. They did not want to give up the power they had gotten from a gun. Jesse James was one of those men.

(Jesse James, Frank James, Cole Younger and BOB YOUNGER enter from right and cross to down center; Jesse motions Cole and Bob Younger to stand at mid center; Jesse and Frank pull bandanas over their faces, draw pistols and confront the surprised Bank Teller.)

MABEL: *(o.s.)* On February 14, 1866, a dozen strangers rode into Liberty, Missouri and spread out around the town square. Shortly after nine a.m., two men burst into the Clay County Savings Association and threatened to kill the teller. They broke open the vault and made off with $60,000 in currency, gold and silver.

(SOUND: gun shots, thundering horses; Jesse and Frank James dash to down center as Bank Teller raises the alarm; LIBERTY BYSTANDER enters from right and also shouts, waving his arms hysterically.)

LIBERTY BANK TELLER: The bank's been robbed! Help! Help!
LIBERTY BYSTANDER: Robbers! Somebody get the sheriff! Get the sheriff!

(Cole and Bob Younger dash offstage up left, followed by Jesse and Frank James; before he exits, Jesse turns and shoots the Bystander, who falls and dies.)

MABEL: *(o.s.)* Besides the bold theft — it was the first robbery of a bank in the United States during daylight — there was blood that day in the streets of Liberty. An innocent bystander, a 19-year-old student at nearby Jewell College, was killed by one of the departing bandits.

(MUSIC: "Jesse James" sung offstage; Two Lawrence Citizens carry Bystander offstage left.)

SINGER *(SINGS)*
    He roamed all over Kansas and Missouri
    At robbing banks Jesse was a clever hand
    He never had to face a trial by jury
    And soon became the leader of his band

    With his brother Frank he robbed the Liberty bank
    And carried the money from the town
    It was in this very place they had a little race
    And shot George Wymore to the ground

HARV: *(o.s.)* For the next few years bank robberies raged throughout Missouri and neighboring states. Jesse and his gang struck at Lexington, Savannah, Richmond and Gallatin, Missouri... Russellville and Columbia, Kentucky...Corydon, Iowa. A teller was killed in Gallatin, a bank president murdered in Russellville, a cashier cut down in Columbia...the James Gang left a bloody trail that became the talk of the nation.

(REPORTER #1 enters from right; REPORTER #2 enters from left; they meet at down center, scribbling onto notepads.)

REPORTER #1: Special to the *Police Gazette*! Kansas City, September 26th, 1872. The Jesse James Gang commit their most daring crime yet — robbing the ticket office of the Kansas City Fair in broad daylight! A small girl is shot in the leg by a richocheting bullet as the bandits flee.

REPORTER #2: An exclusive report in *Harper's Weekly*! On July 21st, 1873, the James Brothers rob a train outside Adair, Iowa. The bandits loosen a rail and wreck the engine — the engineer is trapped in the cab and scalded to death...a young fireman badly burned!

REPORTER #1: Upon leaving, the leader of the thieves announces to the passengers, "We are the boys who are hard to handle, and we will make it hot for the boys who try to take us."

REPORTER #2: And he gives a silver dollar to the conductor, saying: "Take this and drink to the health of Jesse James."

REPORTER #1: Yet many folks refuse to condemn the gang. Some see Jesse as a modern-day Robin Hood, robbing the rich Northern banks to help the suffering Southern poor.

REPORTER #2: When the gang robbed a stage coach near Hot Springs, Arkansas, they gave one passenger his watch and money back because the man proved he had fought for the South during the Civil War.

REPORTER #1: Others say Jesse checks the hands of victims for signs of manual labor. If your hands are rough and callused, it means you are a hard worker, and Jesse won't take your money.

REPORTER #2: And then there's the story of the time Jesse robbed a bank and gave the money to a Confederate widow to pay her mortgage. The banker came and collected the money; when he started back for town, the James Gang was waiting for him and robbed him — stealing the same money twice!

REPORTER #1: Yet despite all the tales of the bandit gang's generosity, Robert Pinkerton of the Pinkerton Detective Agency calls Jesse James "the worst man, without exception, in America. He is utterly devoid of fear and has no more compunction about cold-blooded muder than he has about eating his breakfast."

REPORTER #2: And cold-blooded murder was the order of the day when the James Gang rode into Northfield, Minnesota on September 7th, 1876.

(Reporters #1 and #2 exit right; NORTHFIELD BANK TELLER enters from left and sits on chair behind table at down left; Northfield BANK CUSTOMER enters from left and stands at the table, presenting a bag of coins for deposit; Jesse James, Frank James, Cole Younger, Bob Younger, BILL CHADWELL and CLELL MILLER enter from right and cross slowly to down center; Jesse motions Cole Younger, Chadwell and Miller to stand at mid center; Jesse, Frank and Bob Younger

pull bandanas over their faces, draw pistols and confront the surprised Bank Teller and Customer.)

HARV: *(o.s.)* The gang had been drinking whiskey that morning; they were mean and trigger-happy. When Jesse, Frank and Bob Younger entered the bank, they pulled guns on the cashier, Joseph Heywood. Heywood told them the safe had a time lock and could not be opened for another hour. The bluff worked, and the outlaws left without a cent — but it cost the brave Heywood his life.

(Jesse and Bob Younger run to mid center and join others gang members; Bank Teller stands behind table; Frank James turns and shoots Bank Teller; Bank Teller dies; Frank James blows smoke off his gun, then strolls to mid center. SOUND: gun shot.)

HARV: *(o.s.)* According to witnesses, Frank James turned before leaving the bank and pointed his pistol at Heywood's head — then fired and shot him right between the eyes.

NORTHFIELD BANK CUSTOMER: Help! The bank's being robbed!

(THREE NORTHFIELD CITIZENS enter from right, armed with rifles; Bank Customer points to the gang.)

MABEL: *(o.s.)* The gang had not only chosen the wrong bank, they'd chosen the wrong town. Northfield was home to many men who had fought on the Union side in the Civil War. They still had their guns, and they weren't afraid to use them — especially on renegade Rebels.

(Brief gun battle erupts between James Gang and Northfield Citizens; Chadwell and Miller are killed; Bob Younger is seriously wounded and stumbles offstage up right behind Jesse, Frank and Cole; the Northfield Citizens and Bank Customer exit down right, dragging off Chadwell, Miller and Bank Teller.)

MABEL: *(o.s.)* Chadwell and Miller were killed fleeing the scene; Bob Younger was seriously wounded. Five days later the gang was surrounded and all captured — except for Frank and Jesse, who managed to escape.

HARV: (o.s.) The brothers lay low for nearly three years, eluding a nationwide search. Of course, no one really knew what they looked like. Frank and Jesse were said to be seen in Mexico, California, even New York. Most of the time they lived quietly with their families outside of Nashville, Tennessee, going about their daily business under false names.

(D.L. BLIGH enters from right and sits on table at left, reading a newspaper; Jesse James enters from left, tips his hat and sits next to him; they chat briefly, then Jesse moves to down left exits.)

HARV: (o.s.) One day in Louisville, Jesse saw a famous detective D.L. Bligh, who had been on his trail for years. They chatted amiably for several minutes, without Bligh once suspecting the identity of his acquaintance. The next day the detective received a note.

(D.L. Bligh pulls out note from his pocket and reads it.)

JESSE JAMES: "Dear Mr. Bligh: You have been quoted as saying on more than one occasion that if you could only meet Jesse James, you'd be content to lie down and die. Well, Mr. Bligh, you can now stretch out, lie down and die. The gentleman you met the other day in the Louisville railroad depot was — Yours sincerely, Jesse Woodson James."

(Jesse smiles and exits left; D.L. Bligh crumples note.)

D.L. BLIGH: Bah! That scoundrel! Jesse James, your outlaw days are numbered! (stomps offstage left)

(MUSIC: "Jesse James" sung offstage.)

SINGER (SINGS)
   Now after years of hanging around with outlaws
   Jesse met up with a gent named Robert Ford
   This traitor, though he didn't care about the laws,
   He knew on Jesse's head was a reward
MABEL: (o.s.) In 1879 Jesse and Frank reformed their gang and began robbing banks and trains throughout the mid-South. But folks had grown tired of their blood-thirsty antics, and public opinion turned against the brothers. In July, 1881,

Missouri Governor Thomas Crittenden issued a five thousand dollar reward for Jesse and Frank James — five thousand dollars each, dead or alive. And there were no lack of takers.

(Jesse James enters from left and sits at table; he begins shuffling a deck of cards.)

HARV: *(o.s.)* In November, 1881, Jesse rented a seven-room house in St. Joseph, Missouri, under the alias of Thomas Howard. His wife, Zerelda, and two children — Jesse, Junior and Mary — were with him also. So was a boarder, a man named Charlie Ford, who along with his brother, Robert, had taken part in several recent robberies with Jesse and Frank. On the morning of April 3, 1882, Jesse was planning a robbery for the next day.

(CHARLIE FORD enters from left.)

JESSE JAMES: Charlie Ford! Sit down and play a hand or two!

CHARLIE FORD: *(sits)* Thanks, Jesse. Any more word on the Platte City job?

JESSE JAMES: I've just about got it worked out. We'll meet at — why, thank you, darling!

(Jesse pauses as Mrs. Jesse James enters from left with a cup and saucer; she sets them on table in front of Jesse.)

CHARLIE FORD: *(tips hat)* Good morning, Mrs. James, er, Mrs. Howard. *(chuckles)*

MRS. JESSE JAMES: *(curtly)* Good morning, Mr. Ford. *(crosses to down center and addresses audience)* I never liked Charlie Ford, nor his brother, Robert. Why, Robert Ford had once bragged that he wanted to be the man who killed Jesse James! But Jesse wouldn't listen to me at all. He said the Fords were as good as family; he even gave Robert Ford a gun!

(ROBERT FORD enters from left, wearing a pistol at his side, and stands next to table to left of Jesse.)

JESSE JAMES: You know, boys, I've gotten too old for this trade. Tomorrow's run will be my last. I'm going to take Mrs. James and the children to Nebraska. Buy a little farm in Franklin County and retire. It's time to turn my life around and start fresh.

(Charles and Robert Ford exchange nervous glances.)

JESSE JAMES: You boys feeling all right?

(Charles and Robert Ford nod their heads "yes" as Jesse stares at them.)

CHARLES & ROBERT FORD: Sure, Jesse, er, Mr. Howard, um, sure, we're all right.

MRS. JESSE JAMES: Jesse knew the Fords were up to something. But he figured he'd take care of them the next day, when he met up with Frank. He never got the chance.

(Jesse rises and points to mid center.)

JESSE JAMES: Reckon I'll help Mrs. James with the housework. *(pulls handkerchief from back pocket and mimes dusting a picture, turning his back to the Fords)* Don't tell her I'm making her pictures crooked.

(Charlie and Robert Ford look at each other, Charlie motioning Robert to pull his pistol; Robert Ford pulls his pistol, aims at Jesse's head and shoots. SOUND: gun shot. Jesse falls to floor as Mrs. Jesse James turns and kneels at Jesse's side.)

ROBERT FORD: It was an accident!

MRS. JESSE JAMES: An accident on purpose! You traitor! Robert Ford, traitor! May you and your brother never know a moment of peace!

(Charlie and Robert Ford dash offstage left; LIGHTS OUT; MUSIC: "Jesse James" sung offstage.)

SINGER: *(SINGS)*
Robert Ford walked into the room that fateful morning
While Jesse was dusting pictures in their frames
He shot him in the back without a warning
And that's the end of Mr. Jesse James

(LIGHTS UP FULL on the bus station interior; Harv and Freddie sit on the bench; Mabel stands behind podium; Elmer sweeps the floor at down center.)

HARV: Frank James surrendered six months later. He was tried for two of the gang's robberies and acquitted both times for lack of evidence. He lived until 1915, working at odd jobs and operating a museum on his farm.

FREDDIE: What about the Fords? Did they get their reward?

MABEL: You could say so. Charlie Ford committed suicide two years later. And Robert was killed in a gunfight in Colorado in 1892 by a man who wanted to kill the man who killed Jesse James.

FREDDIE: Then Jesse James is definitely dead?

HARV: If you trust the word of those lying scoundrel Ford brothers. The only other witness was Jesse's wife.

MABEL: Who might have reason to conceal her husband's *real* whereabouts.

FREDDIE: But it's so incredible! Jesse James — still alive?

HARV: Jesse was a master of disguise. He could have paid the Fords to say they killed him and still be wandering the country today.

MABEL: He could be anywhere.

HARV: He could be anybody.

FREDDIE: Anybody?

MABEL: Even old Elmer over there. He'd be about the right age, wouldn't he?

(Freddie, Harv and Mabel look at Elmer intently for a moment, then burst out laughing; Mabel and Harv exit right and Freddie reads newspaper. Elmer sweeps along toward offstage right, whistling "Jesse James"; he stops in front of Freddie.)

ELMER: Got something for you, sonny. *(hands Freddie a silver dollar, winks)*

FREDDIE: A silver dollar?

ELMER: You and your college friends can take this...and drink to the health of Jesse James.

(Elmer sweeps offstage right as Freddie stares open-mouthed at coin in his hand and at the departing Elmer.)

FREDDIE: Well, I'll be a banana split!

(LIGHTS OUT; MUSIC: "Jesse James" sung offstage; Entire Cast joins on chorus.)

SINGER *(SINGS)*
 So good folks, what's the use of us pretending
 It doesn't pay to play those crooked games
 Beware of any such unhappy ending
 Just profit by the death of Jesse James
ENTIRE CAST: *(SINGS)*
 Jesse left a wife to mourn for his life
 Three children, sad and brave
 But the dirty little coward that shot Mr. Howard
 Has laid Jesse James in his grave

THE END

Jesse James
(traditional, arranged by L.E. McCullough)

You've heard of ban- dits brave in all their glo- ry; in his- to- ry you've of- ten read their names; But lend an ear and you will hear the sto- ry a- bout that fa- mous ban- dit Jes- se James.

Jes- se left a wife to mourn for his life, three chil- dren sad and brave; But the dir- ty lit- tle co- ward that shot Mis- ter Ho- ward has laid Jes-se James in his grave

NINTH CAVALRY TO THE RESCUE!

In 1866, the U.S. Congress passed a law directing the Army to create four regiments of African-American cavalry and infantry for service on the Western Plains — the first African-American soldiers commissioned to serve during peacetime. However, the 9th and 10th Cavalry and 24th and 25th Infantry regiments saw little peace; after a few months training at Fort Leavenworth, Kansas, they were immediately sent out to pacify hostile Indian tribes driven to the warpath by treaty-breaking white settlers. The Indians called them "Buffalo Soldiers," and during the next three decades, some 6,000 Buffalo Soldiers helped bring order to the Wild West, making up twenty per cent of the soldiers who fought in the Indian Wars of the late 1800s. General Colin Powell, the nation's first African-American four-star general, served as deputy commander of Fort Leavenworth in 1981–82; in 1992 he spoke at the dedication of Buffalo Soldier Monument and gave a stirring tribute to the Buffalo Soldiers' legacy of service.

TIME: July 25, 1992; 1870s–'80s

PLACE: Fort Leavenworth, Kansas

RUNNING TIME: 20 minutes

CAST: 24 actors, min. 7 boys

General Colin Powell
Corporal William Wilson
Sergeant George Jordan
4 Cowboys
Governor Lew Wallace
6 Sioux Warriors

Announcer
Sergeant Thomas Shaw
2 Cavalry Soldiers
Billy the Kid
Wovoka
4 Apache Warriors

115

STAGE SET: podium at down right; large rock at mid center; large rock at mid left

PROPS: 4 rifles, 4 pistols, letter, rope, Medal of Honor

EFFECTS: Sound — crowd applause; gun shots; cavalry bugle blowing "Charge!"; door knocking; Indian drum beats

MUSIC: *Ghost Dance Song, Sometimes I Feel Like a Motherless Child*

COSTUMES: General Colin Powell wears modern military dress suit with medals and hat; Cavalry and Buffalo Soldiers wear dark blue shirts and black or brown pants, black or brown knee boots, beige or brown Stetson hats and other Cavalry accessories such as canteens, cartridge belts, gloves; Sioux and Apache Warriors wear battle costume, with Sioux wearing more buckskin, feathers and war paint than Apaches, who dress simpler; Wovoka dresses similar to Sioux Warriors but with more of a chief's accessories such as a pendant or blanket

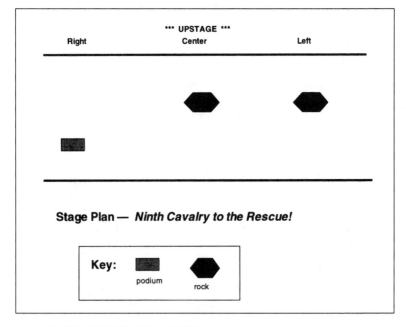

*** UPSTAGE ***

Right — Center — Left

Stage Plan — *Ninth Cavalry to the Rescue!*

Key: podium rock

(SPOTLIGHT RIGHT on a podium at down right, where GENERAL COLIN POWELL stands, facing audience; an ANNOUNCER'S voice sounds from offstage.)

ANNOUNCER: *(o.s.)* Welcome, ladies and gentlemen, to Fort Leavenworth, Kansas. Here, presiding over today's dedication ceremony of the Buffalo Soldier Monument, is General Colin Powell, Chairman of the Chiefs of Staff of the United States Armed Forces.

(SOUND: crowd applause fades up then out.)

GENERAL COLIN POWELL: Today — July 25, 1992 — we remember an important date in American history. Exactly 126 years ago, Congress passed a law that created four regiments of African-American troops with orders to fight in the Wild West. These troops served on the frontier for over 30 years. Because of their unyielding bravery and rugged appearance, their Indian foes called them "Buffalo Soldiers." This statue by renowned sculptor Eddie Dixon celebrates the eighteen African-American soldiers who won the Congressional Medal of Honor while serving on the Great Plains.

(SPOTLIGHT LEFT on CORPORAL WILLIAM WILSON standing at parade rest at down left; General Colin Powell gestures to left.)

GENERAL COLIN POWELL: Look at him. Soldier of the nation. Eagles on his buttons, crossed sabres on his canteen, a rifle in his hand, a pistol on his hip. He was every bit the soldier his white brother was. He showed that the theory of inequality must be wrong. He could not be denied his right. It might take time; it did take time. But he knew that in the end he could not be denied.

(SPOTLIGHT OUT on General Colin Powell; LIGHTS UP LEFT on Corporal William Wilson, who snaps to attention and addresses audience.)

CORPORAL WILLIAM WILSON: Corporal William Wilson, Ninth United States Cavalry, sir! *(salutes sharply)* At ease, yes sir! *(stands at ease)* My Medal of Honor? I got it for bravery during the battle at Pine Ridge Reservation, South Dakota,

December 30, 1890. We — that is, the Ninth Cavalry — had just ridden up to reinforce the Seventh Cavalry — that's right, George Custer's old outfit — when all of a sudden, arrows came from everywhere! Hold on, I'm getting ahead of myself again. Maybe I better start back at the beginning.

(MUSIC UP as LIGHTS UP LEFT AND CENTER on FOUR ARMED COWBOYS, two at mid center and two at mid left shooting at each other from behind large rocks. MUSIC: "Sometimes I Feel Like a Motherless Child" played as uptempo march one time through then out.)

CORPORAL WILLIAM WILSON: Folks today think all we did is fight Indians. That wasn't the case, though we did see our share of war paint and tomahawks. But when I first joined the regiment in 1878, we were in southern New Mexico — Lincoln County — right smack dab in the middle of a fullscale range war between cattle barons.

(SOUND: five seconds of gun shots exchanged between Armed Cowboys, then a cavalry bugle blowing "Charge! as TWO CAVALRY SOLDIERS enter from left and point rifles at cowboys.)

CAVALRY SOLDIER #1: Both sides, cease firing at once!

(Cowboys cease firing, look quizzically at soldiers.)

CAVALRY SOLDIER #2: Under authority of the United States Army, martial law is hereby declared in Lincoln County! Get back to your homes and places of business at once!

(Cowboys reluctantly rise and stagger offstage, left and right respectively; Cavalry Soldiers follow them offstage with rifles pointed and exit.)

CORPORAL WILLIAM WILSON: Even with the cavalry on the scene, both gangs kept up the feuding. Things got so bad, President Hayes fired the New Mexico governor and sent in a new one — General Lew Wallace from Indiana.

(GOVERNOR LEW WALLACE enters from right and stands at down center, reading a letter.)

CORPORAL WILLIAM WILSON: This fellow Wallace had fought in the Civil War and saved Washington, D.C. from Jubal Early and the Confederates. Now, he was determined to clean up the Lincoln County range war by asking assistance from one of the main combatants — William Bonney — better known as Billy the Kid.

GOVERNOR LEW WALLACE: *(reading)* W.H. Bonney...come to the house of Squire Wilson at nine o'clock Monday night alone. I have the authority to exempt you from prosecution, if you will testify to what you say you know. Signed, Governor Lew Wallace, New Mexico Territory

(SOUND: knocking on door.)

GOVERNOR LEW WALLACE: *(looks to right)* Come in!

(Cradling a rifle in his arms, BILLY THE KID enters from right, stepping stealthily out of the shadows and circling behind Governor Lew Wallace, coming to stand at the Governor's left, rifle still at the ready.)

BILLY THE KID: Your note gave me promise of protection.

GOVERNOR LEW WALLACE: I have kept my bargain, Mr. Bonney. Now you keep yours. This turmoil must end. Testify before the grand jury as state's witness so we can convict the ringleaders.

BILLY THE KID: If I testify, I will be dead within hours.

GOVERNOR LEW WALLACE: The army will protect you. The Ninth Cavalry are among the best troops in the West.

BILLY THE KID: *(lowers rifle)* Billy the Kid lets his bullets do the talking. But I reckon I can give words a try this once. See you at the courthouse, Governor. *(exits quickly left; Governor Lew Wallace exits right.)*

CORPORAL WILLIAM WILSON: Rough as outlaws like Billy the Kid might be, the toughest scraps we had were with Apaches. In 1880 we'd chased Victorio and his warrior band across three thousand miles of burning desert, until he crossed into Mexico. The next year, the Apache chief Nana led his tribe into battle. The Buffalo Soldiers were the first line of defense.

(MUSIC: "Sometimes I Feel Like a Motherless Child" played slowly as SERGEANT THOMAS SHAW and SERGEANT

GEORGE JORDAN enter from right and join Wilson at down left; the soldiers crouch in a semi-circle facing audience, with rifles and pistols at the ready, as if expecting imminent attack.)

SERGEANT THOMAS SHAW: Sergeant Jordan, if I remember correctly, our Sunday-school book told us it is wrong to persecute the poor Indian. Weren't they here first?

SERGEANT GEORGE JORDAN: Of course it's wrong, Sergeant Shaw. But if I remember correctly, there is a whole pack of Apaches out there interested in persecuting us right out of our skin. As the Golden Rule in my Sunday-school book said, "Do unto others *before* they do unto you."

CORPORAL WILLIAM WILSON: Think about it, gentlemen. Here we are — hired to hunt and kill red men, when black and brown men like ourselves are being killed all over the South by lynch mobs and the Ku Klux Klan.

SERGEANT GEORGE JORDAN: That's true, Corporal Wilson. But if you were in Dixie right now, you wouldn't be able to do much except swing in the breeze. Out here, you have the chance to prove yourself the best fighting cavalryman in the world. Nobody can take that away from you...not now, not ever.

(SOUND: three gun shots, Apache war whoops.)

SERGEANT THOMAS SHAW: *(points right)* Here they come!

(FOUR APACHES enter from up right and dash behind rocks at mid center and left, firing at the soldiers, who lie at down left and return fire. SOUND: several gun shots, Apache war whoops.)

SERGEANT GEORGE JORDAN: They're trying to surround us! Wilson, get back to the captain and tell him to bring up the command!

(Wilson stands and moves a few feet to the left; gun shots and war whoops cease; Apaches slip offstage up right; Shaw and Jordan stand, gaze after the exiting Apaches and exit offstage left.)

CORPORAL WILLIAM WILSON: Though exposed and outnumbered, Sergeant Thomas Shaw and Sergeant George Jordan held off the attack until reinforcements arrived. For their bravery that day at Carizzo Canyon, both were awarded the Congressional Medal of Honor.

(FOUR APACHES enter from right, chained together with rope around their waists; followed by TWO CAVALRY SOLDIERS, they march slowly to center stage, where they stop.)

CORPORAL WILLIAM WILSON: In 1886, the Buffalo Soldiers helped round up the Apache warrior Geronimo at Skeleton Canyon in Arizona. That was the end of the Indian Wars in the Southwest.

APACHE #1: *(faces audience)* I will quit the warpath and live at peace hereafter. I don't want that we should be killing each other. Once I moved about like the wind. Now I surrender to you, and that is all.

(APACHES and SOLDIERS march slowly across stage and exit left; TWO ARMED COWBOYS enter from right, creeping onstage as if they are secretly following the APACHES and SOLDIERS.)

CORPORAL WILLIAM WILSON: The defeated Apaches were marched to a railroad depot and then shipped to a prison in Florida. Not only did we have to make sure the Indians didn't escape, the Buffalo Soldiers had to keep watch on a group of vengeful cowboys who followed behind — waiting for the chance to kill any Apache man, woman or child they could.

(SOLDIER #2 threatens COWBOYS with his rifle; COWBOYS back off and exit right.)

CORPORAL WILLIAM WILSON: Besides subduing hostile Indians — and then protecting them — we troopers had plenty run-of-the-mill peacekeeping to do. We escorted payroll stages, carried the mail, helped stranded travelers. I must have strung up a hundred miles of telegraph poles and built I don't know how many log stockades! And for $13 a month! In 1888, the famous Western artist Frederic Remington rode with a troop of Buffalo Soldiers on a scouting trip in New Mexico. Remington was writing an article for *Harper's Weekly* magazine, and we gave him plenty to write about!

(SOUND: Indian drum beat offstage; FOUR SIOUX WAR-RIORS enter from right and cross slowly to mid center, where they hold hands in a semi-circle facing audience.)

CORPORAL WILLIAM WILSON: But it was at Pine Ridge, South Dakota that I won my medal in 1890. Yes, after all these years, I can still hear the drums of the Sioux Ghost Dancers...and I can still hear the Ghost Dance Song.

(MUSIC: "Ghost Dance Song" sung by FOUR SIOUX WARRIORS.)

FOUR SIOUX WARRRIORS: *(SING)*
Father, have pity on me
I am crying for thirst
All is gone
I have nothing to eat

The day is coming
The day is coming
The day is coming

The Father will descend
The earth will tremble
The buffalo will return
The white man will disappear

The day is coming
The day is coming
The day is coming

(Drumming continues through ensuing dialogue, picking up tempo and volume as battle begins.)

CORPORAL WILLIAM WILSON: A new religion had started among the tribes of the Plains. It was called the Ghost Dance, and its prophet was a Paiute shaman named Wovoka. He and his followers believed the Indians could dance the white man away.

(WOVOKA enters from right and stands at down center, facing audience.)

WOVOKA: The earth is getting old, and I will make it new for my chosen people — the Indians.
FOUR SIOUX WARRIORS: The day is coming!

WOVOKA: I will cover the earth with new soil, which will bury all the white people.

FOUR SIOUX WARRIORS: The day is coming!

WOVOKA: My new earth will be covered with sweet grass, and the buffalo herds will return, and my Indian children will roam freely over it. The day is coming!

FOUR SIOUX WARRIORS: The day is coming!

WOVOKA: Aaiiiiiieeee!

(Wovoka dashes offstage right; FOUR SIOUX WARRIORS begin dancing at mid center as drumming picks up speed and volume.)

CORPORAL WILLIAM WILSON: As the winter got colder, all the Sioux chiefs joined the Ghost Dancers: Short Bull, Good Thunder, Catch the Bear and Sitting Bull. They wore special "ghost shirts" they believed would stop the white man's bullets. Men, women and children danced in the snow and freezing wind all through the day and night. The reservation agents became scared and called in the Ninth Cavalry. We came...and waited.

(Drumming and dancing stop; FOUR SIOUX WARRIORS freeze in position.)

CORPORAL WILLIAM WILSON: On December 15th, a group of reservation police decided to capture the Ghost Dancers. They went to Sitting Bull's lodge — and killed him.

(SOUND: a gun shot; SIOUX WARRIOR #1 falls dead.)

CORPORAL WILLIAM WILSON: Terrified the police would kill them next, the other chiefs took their people from the reservation and fled into the Badlands. The Seventh Cavalry was sent to bring them back. On December 29th, they found a group of 120 men and 230 women and children resting at Wounded Knee Creek. All of a sudden, trouble started and shooting began.

(SOUND: several gun shots; SIOUX WARRIORS #2, 3 & 4 fall dead.)

CORPORAL WILLIAM WILSON: It was a massacre. Within half an

hour, 300 Sioux lay dead, shot where they stood in the freezing snow, their ghost shirts red with blood.

(SIOUX WARRIORS #5 & 6 rush onstage from right and hide behind large rocks at mid center and mid left.)

CORPORAL WILLIAM WILSON: Other tribes heard the gun fire and raced out from the reservation, attacking the Seventh Cavalry and pinning them down. The message came to the Ninth Cavalry: stop the fighting and rescue the troopers!

(SOUND: cavalry bugle blowing "Charge!" and several gun shots as SIOUX WARRIORS #5 & 6 fire at CORPORAL WILSON, who ducks.)

CORPORAL WILLIAM WILSON: I was in the advance scouting party. Two miles from Wounded Knee, we came under fire. Private Haywood was killed in the first volley. Our captain asked for a volunteer to ride back and tell the main troop to come up fast. I volunteered.

(CORPORAL WILSON moves, crouched, toward down center, as SIOUX WARRIORS #5 & 6 fire at him. SOUND: gun shots.)

CORPORAL WILLIAM WILSON: Two warriors tried to cut me off, but my horse outran them. I made it to the troop, and the Captain led us back in two columns — one column to the east, one column to the west.

(TWO CAVALRY SOLDIERS enter from right and follow CORPORAL WILSON as he moves forward, firing at SIOUX WARRIORS #5 & 6; SOUND: gun shots. WARRIORS are shot and fall to ground; TWO CAVALRY SOLDIERS drag them offstage up left and exit as CORPORAL WILSON crosses to down left.)

CORPORAL WILLIAM WILSON: The Ninth Cavalry turned the tide, and the Sioux surrendered. It was the last battle of the Indian Wars...and one of the saddest of them all. *(pulls medal out of his pocket and shows it to audience)* They gave me this Congressional Medal of Honor for my fast riding that day — "bravery under fire." Eight years later during the Spanish-American War, the Buffalo Soldiers won five more Medals when they helped save Teddy Roosevelt's Rough Riders at San Juan Hill.

(SOUND: cavalry bugle blowing "Charge!.")

CORPORAL WILLIAM WILSON: After that war, the Army didn't have much use for cavalry. The Buffalo Soldiers retired, one by one. Would you believe, we were the last men on horseback in the entire United States Army! Well, maybe it was because — to us Buffalo Soldiers, anyway — the world looked a little bit better from up on a saddle. *(snaps to attention as first two bars of "Sometimes I Feel Like a Motherless Child" are played slowly offstage.)*

(SPOTLIGHT RIGHT ON GENERAL COLIN POWELL at podium, addressing audience.)

GENERAL COLIN POWELL: The Buffalo Soldier believed that hatred and bigotry and prejudice could not defeat him. He believed that through his pain and sacrifice, future generations would know full freedom. And today, we know he was right. I challenge every young person here: don't forget their service and their sacrifice. Be an eagle — and soar!

(CORPORAL WILSON salutes and smiles. CHORUS offstage sings "Sometimes I Feel Like a Motherless Child" as uptempo march. LIGHTS FADE OUT.)

CHORUS: *(SINGS)*
Sometimes I feel like a motherless child
Sometimes I feel like a motherless child
Sometimes I feel like a motherless child
A long ways from home

Sometimes I feel like I'm almost gone
Sometimes I feel like I'm almost gone
Sometimes I feel like I'm almost gone
A long ways from home

Sometimes I feel like a feather in the wind
Sometimes I feel like a feather in the wind
Sometimes I feel like a feather in the wind
A long ways from home

THE END

Ghost Dance Song
(words: traditional, music: L.E. McCullough)

Fa- ther, have pi- ty on me; I am cry- ing for thirst. All is gone; I have no- thing to eat The day is co- ming! The day is co- ming! The day is co- ming! The Fa- ther will de- scend; the earth will trem- ble; The bu- ffa- lo will re- turn; the white man will dis- a- ppear. The day is co- ming! The day is co- ming! The day is

music © L.E. McCullough 1997

Cavalry Call: "Charge!"
(traditional, arranged by L.E. McCullough)

Sometimes I Feel Like a Motherless Child
— march tempo — (traditional, arr. by L.E. McCullough)

Some-times I feel like a mo-ther-less child;

Some-times I feel like a mo-ther-less child;

Some-times I feel like a mo-ther-less child; a

long wa———ys from home

Sometimes I Feel Like a Motherless Child
— slow tempo — (traditional, arr. by L.E. McCullough)

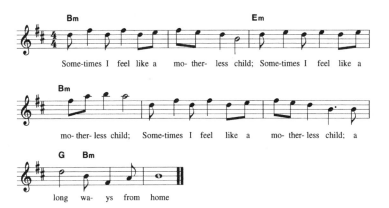

Some-times I feel like a mo-ther-less child; Some-times I feel like a

mo-ther-less child; Some-times I feel like a mo-ther-less child; a

long wa-ys from home

OUTLAW GOLD:
THE LOST TREASURE OF COMMANCHE CREEK

It seems like nearly every county in the West is home to a legend concerning a lost mine or buried outlaw treasure. Additionally, most of the legends center around classic plots of treachery and murder, thieves turning on each other as they greedily succumb to the allure of boundless wealth. Are any of these treasure stories true? Certainly, many great fortunes were stolen and "misplaced" during the lawless days of the frontier West — few were ever recovered or accounted for. Maybe there's one not far from you...

TIME: Last year about this time

PLACE: Somewhere in the West

RUNNING TIME: 20 minutes

CAST: 9 actors, min. 4 boys, 3 girls

Janis	Karen
Phillip	Bloody Bill Crow
Maggie Phelps	Bonaparte Phelps
Shreveport	2 Commanches

STAGE SET: a large sitting rock at down right and one at down left; another taller rock at up center; a few bricks and small boards scattered at mid left

PROPS: hardback book, folded-up piece of paper, flashlight, knapsack, divining stick, knife, 2 pistols, rope, shovel, spear, tomahawk, Mexican gold peso

EFFECTS: Sound — Indian drums, a coyote howl, gun shots

COSTUMES: Janis, Karen and Phillip dress as contemporary pre-
teens; Bonaparte Phelps dresses in a flannel shirt and jeans and
gives the appearance he might be contemporary; other characters
wear standard 1860s frontier dress

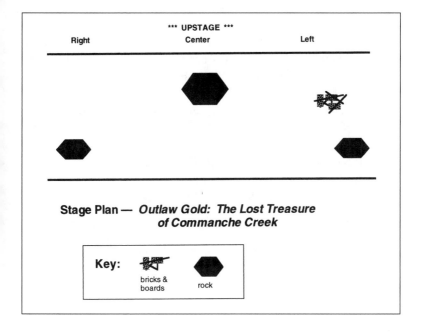

Stage Plan — *Outlaw Gold: The Lost Treasure
of Commanche Creek*

*(LIGHTS UP RIGHT on JANIS sitting on a large rock at down
right; she is leafing through a hardback book, looks up and
addresses audience.)*

JANIS: Hi. My name's Janis. I don't know if I'm a typical American
kid, because I don't care much for computers or video games.
I'd rather sit in the library reading old books. But I *do* know I
love a good adventure. And *that's* what happened when I found
this book about our town's history.

(KAREN and PHILLIP enter from right and greet JANIS.)

KAREN: Hi, Janis!

PHILLIP: What's up?

JANIS: *(jumps up excitedly)* Karen, Phillip! I found the most amazing story in this book! Stolen treasure and outlaws and a massacre and poisoned arrows and-and-and-and big flaming death!

PHILLIP: Hey, slow down! School starts Monday, and my brain is already on overdrive. One new thought per hour, okay?

KAREN: Just start from the top.

JANIS: Okay. Back in March, 1865, just one month before the Civil War ended, a Confederate army squad was ambushed down by Commanche Creek. There wasn't even any town here then, just a one-room cabin used as a shelter by trappers when they came through looking for game.

KAREN: Who ambushed the army squad? Union soldiers?

JANIS: No. It was a band of outlaws who found out the Confederates were carrying a load of gold — Spanish gold that had been taken from a church vault in Mexico.

PHILLIP: Let me continue. The outlaws courteously returned the missing gold to the church and were given lifetime passes to Taco Bell.

KAREN: Phillip!

JANIS: The Indians who lived here back then were on the warpath, and the outlaws decided to bury the gold near the cabin and meet again in three months to take their shares. But, according to this book, *none* of the outlaws ever made it back. They all died terrible deaths, and the gold has never found — to this very day.

KAREN: And you think you're the only person who knows about the buried treasure? Janis, look at that old book. *(opens the back cover and points to the inside)* You can see it's been taken out a dozen times! Surely somebody else has gone looking for the gold!

JANIS: I'm sure they have. But I bet they didn't have this little item.

(Janis produces a folded-up piece of paper and shows it to Karen and Phillip.)

KAREN: You found a treasure map in the book!

JANIS: Nope. I found a poem.

KAREN: *(pause)* Excuse me, girlfriend, but are we on the same rinse cycle? You found a *poem*?

PHILLIP: A po-em! A po-em! The lady found a po-em!

KAREN: *(takes the paper)* Was it, like, just sitting in the book staring at you?

JANIS: As if! *That's* not the poem. That's just what I copied it on. *(carefully leafs through book)* But the poem is *in* the book. See? Every twelve pages, there's one word underlined somewhere on the page. When you put the words together in sequence, they make a poem.

KAREN: *(reads paper):*
The sparkling shores that crimson climb
Inflame the dark noon hour
Where shaded by the eagle's claw
Bright rays of carrot flower

PHILLIP: I have a better poem. "Roses are red, violets are plain; if you listen to her, you're completely insane."

JANIS: Look, guys, it's simple. "Sparkling shores" are the banks of Commanche Creek. The "crimson climb" means it's right by Red Mesa.

KAREN: Red Mesa Mall?

JANIS: No! Red Mesa *mesa*! About a mile *past* the mall, Commanche Creek flows right up to the base of the Red Mesa rock formation.

KAREN: Wow, I always wondered what that big rock thingie was. I thought it was an old Flintstones theme park.

PHILLIP: Pardon me, madame poet. "Inflame the dark noon hour"?

JANIS: Midnight is also known as "dark noon." At midnight the moonlight will reflect off the creek and shine into the cabin. Come on, I'll explain the rest on the way!

KAREN: You're not thinking of going out there?

JANIS: Hey, I know this sounds a little wacky, but it's the last Saturday of summer. What else have we got to do tonight?

PHILLIP: We could do something intelligent and responsible — like sleep.

KAREN: I promised I'd help my parents program the VCR.

JANIS: Oh, come on, you two! We're kids! Grownups always say this is the best time of our lives! Let's have some adventure while we still can!

KAREN: *(pause)* All right. I'm in! What have we got to lose?

(Janis and Karen exit right.)

PHILLIP: Hmmm...*(counts off on fingers)* outlaws, massacres, creepy old cabins at midnight...maybe just our lives. *(shrugs, exits right)*

(LIGHTS OUT BRIEFLY; A FLASHLIGHT shines as Janis, Karen and Phillip enter from right and slowly cross to down center, where they gaze around them; Karen carries a knapsack, Phillip a flashlight, Janis the book; LIGHTS FADE UP CENTER AND LEFT.)

JANIS: I can't believe this old cabin is still standing! It must be almost a hundred fifty years old!

PHILLIP: If you call some old floorboards and a pile of rocks "standing." I doubt it was ever much more than a shack.

KAREN: Wasn't this some kind of worshipping place for the Indians?

JANIS: The Commanches used it as a sacred burial ground. They'd lived in this area since the 1300s.

PHILLIP: That's a lot of buried Indians. Watch where you step.

KAREN: How did the outlaws find this place?

JANIS: Their leader, Bloody Bill Crow, had been a U.S. Army officer before the Civil War, and he knew this part of the country from scouting trips. After a robbery, the gang would come back to Red Mesa and hole up. There's a trail behind the cabin that leads into the rocks.

PHILLIP: Did you say "Bloody" Bill Crow? As in blood, as in gore, as in wounds, as in death?

JANIS: Bloody Bill Crow was such a totally vicious killer, he was kicked out of the Army. He'd even go psycho and attack his own men, if he was in a bad mood.

KAREN: Sounds like a babysitter I once had. But what I want to know is—

JANIS: Watch out!

(LIGHTS FLASH BRIEFLY; Janis, Karen and Phillip duck and crouch.)

PHILLIP: Whaaa!

KAREN: What is it?

JANIS: It's...it's okay. I think it was just a bat.

KAREN: A bat?

JANIS: Red Mesa is full of caves. We should probably watch out for snakes, too.

PHILLIP: Glad I wore my high-tops!

JANIS: *(points to left)* Look! Over there!

(Phillip shines light at down left where YOUNG WOMAN [MAGGIE PHELPS] stands half in shadow.)

JANIS: Hello! Who is it?

MAGGIE: Leave this place at once!

PHILLIP: But we just got here. Say, have you seen any buried — errrff!

(Janis cuts him off with a poke in the ribs.)

PHILLIP: I mean, berries, any berries? We're having a blueberry-picking contest. Wanna help?

MAGGIE: You must leave at once! They're coming! Please, go away!

JANIS: Who? Who is coming?

PHILLIP: Hey-whoa!

(Phillip drops the flashlight; Young Woman exits left quickly; Phillip picks up flashlight and shines it where Maggie had stood.)

JANIS: She's gone!

(Janis walks to down left and searches the ground; Karen paces at down center looking out into audience; Phillip plays flashlight around stage as he walks to mid right.)

PHILLIP: She seemed a bit stressed out.

KAREN: Did you see the way she was dressed? Like it was hoe-down night at the prom!

PHILLIP: I think she's a waitress at the Ponderosa. They always tell me to leave at once, too!

(SOUND: faint Indian drums.)

KAREN: (stops) Do you guys hear something?
PHILLIP: Something rhythmic and drum-like?
KAREN: It must be traffic on the interstate. Or a sonic boom from an airplane.
PHILLIP: (shines flashlight at mid center) How about some angry dead Commanches?

(SPOTLIGHT UP CENTER on TWO COMMANCHES standing partially obscured behind the tall rock; Phillip backs away toward Karen.)

KAREN: Angry Dead Commanches? My friend Sheryl has their new CD. It's really rad!

(Phillip bumps into Karen; SPOTLIGHT OUT; DRUMS STOP; Commanches exit up right.)

KAREN: Hey!
PHILLIP: Sorry! (shines flashlight where Commanches had stood) They're gone!
KAREN: Who's gone?
PHILLIP: The — they were right over — oh, never mind. I'm just way tired, I guess. Or maybe I am asleep, and this is all a dream.
JANIS: Guys! Come here quick!

(Phillip and Karen rush over to mid left where Janis kneels amid a pile of scattered bricks and boards.)

JANIS: What's the third line of the poem?
KAREN: "Where shaded by the eagle's claw"?
JANIS: The Mexican flag has an eagle on it. And the gold was from Mexico. (points at ground) Look at that.
PHILLIP: (shines flashlight) At that piece of wood?
KAREN: It looks like it broke off an old wooden box.
JANIS: Let me rub some of the dirt away. (rubs)
KAREN: An eagle! I see the outline of an eagle!

JANIS: It probably came from one of the boxes the gold was carried in. And was left as a marker to show where the gold is buried.

PHILLIP: What about the last line of the poem? "Bright rays of carrot flower."

JANIS: I'm still pondering about that. But the library has a coin encyclopedia that said early 19th-century Mexican gold coins bore portraits of the King of Spain. The word "king" in Spanish is "rey" — r-e-y. It's a homonym, get it?

KAREN: And "carrot flower"? Were these outlaws, like, vegetarians?

JANIS: Not the carrots you eat. But the c-a-r-a-t carat that measures the weight of gold. And flower, as a verb, means to bloom or to be plentiful.

PHILLIP: Which the gold *would* be.

KAREN: *If* it were buried here.

PHILLIP: Which it's *not*. Because Janis is a certified loony tune who spends way too much time in the library! Come on, let's get outa here!

BONAPARTE PHELPS: Say there, pards, can you shine some of that candle my way?

(SPOTLIGHT UP DOWN RIGHT on an old man, BONAPARTE PHELPS, sitting on the rock and holding a divining stick; Janis, Karen and Phillip whirl around to face him.)

JANIS: Who-who are you?

BONAPARTE PHELPS: Oh, doggone my manners, name's Phelps, Bonaparte Phelps. We don't get many strangers out this way.

PHILLIP: We?

BONAPARTE PHELPS: Me and my daughter, Maggie. Have you seen her pass by? She usually brings me a bite of refreshment long about this time of night. What'd you say your names were?

(Janis crosses to center, followed by Karen and Phillip.)

JANIS: My name is Janis. These are my friends, Karen and Phillip.

BONAPARTE PHELPS: Pleased to meet you. Had any luck finding the treasure?

(Janis, Karen and Phillip exchange glances; Bonaparte Phelps stands and crosses to center.)

BONAPARTE PHELPS: *(chuckles)* Aw, don't give us those long faces. I'm looking for the treasure myself. See this here water-witcher? *(holds up divining rod)* I fixed it so it can signal the whereabouts of gold.

PHILLIP: *(examines rod)* Cool! Where do the batteries go?

JANIS: It doesn't have batteries, Phillip. It's a stick called a "divining rod," and people in the Old West used to think it could locate underground water supplies. They'd even pay traveling con artists called "diviners" huge sums of money to search for water or make the sky rain.

BONAPARTE PHELPS: We'd best work in teams. I'll take this young buck and head that way. You two ladies search over yonder.

KAREN: Ummm, I think we should all stay together in case—

(The rod begins trembling in Phillip's hands, making Phillip shake.)

PHILLIP: It's moving! The witcher-ma-diggit is moving!

(Bonaparte Phelps takes Phillip's right arm.)

BONAPARTE PHELPS: Steady, boy, steady! We're hot on the trail! *(leads Phillip offstage right)* I got a feeling this is gonna be our lucky night! Come on, pard! *(exits right)*

(Phillip hands flashlight to Karen; something offstage left has caught Janis' attention, and she exits offstage left as LIGHTS FADE OUT LEFT AND CENTER.)

KAREN: Phillip, be careful! Oh, this always happens in scary movies! The kids split up, and then the monsters pick them off one by one! Say, Janis, remember that time we— *(turns and can't find Janis)* Janis? Janis! Don't play games! Where are you, Janis? *(moves left with flashlight)* Janis!

JANIS: *(o.s. left)* Over here!

KAREN: And where is here? We're in the middle of a cave, for crying out loud!

(No reply for several seconds.)

KAREN: Janis!!!
BLOODY BILL CROW: She's right here, missy.

(LIGHTS UP LEFT on two men, BLOODY BILL CROW and SHREVEPORT, stand at down left behind Janis, who sits on rock.)

KAREN: Well...hi, everybody! *(waves)*

(Bloody Bill Crow and Shreveport return the wave.)

BLOODY BILL CROW: Good evening. We are so pleased you young ladies can join us.

(Shreveport smiles and beckons Karen forward with his index finger; Karen moves slowly toward them.)

BLOODY BILL CROW: Introductions are in order. My name is William Crow, Captain, United States Army Retired. This is my associate in commerce, Master Shreveport.

(Shreveport smiles at Karen and waves.)

BLOODY BILL CROW: Oh, he cannot speak. The poor devil got his tongue caught on the wrong end of a Bowie knife some years back. But he is very friendly...and very efficient.
KAREN: What exactly is it you do so — efficiently?
BLOODY BILL CROW: We are seekers of fortune, the same as you. Tell me, have you had any luck in your quest?
JANIS: *(stands, addresses Crow)* Listen, you better get as far away from here as you can before my father comes!
BLOODY BILL CROW: *(laughs)* Your father! Darling, there is not a man West of the Mississippi who would throw down on Bloody Bill Crow!
JANIS: Duh! I don't believe you're Bloody Bill Crow! I think you're a couple geeks who followed us when we passed the bus station! Now, bug off!
BLOODY BILL CROW: *(puts his right hand over his heart)* My hand to Hannah! Shreveport, have you ever heard such vile epithets issuing from a maiden's lips?
(Shreveport nods "no"; Crow takes a long knife from inside his jacket and walks around Janis to stand behind Shreveport.)
BLOODY BILL CROW: Perhaps they need a sign.

(Shreveport nods "yes"; Janis and Karen back toward center.)

BLOODY BILL CROW: A certification.

(Shreveport nods "yes.")

BLOODY BILL CROW: A concrete example of my true standing as a treacherous, black-hearted fiend!

(Shreveport nods "yes"; Bloody Bill Crow raises knife and stabs Shreveport in the heart.)

BLOODY BILL CROW: There it is!

(Janis and Karen recoil, hug each other; Shreveport falls to ground, dead; Crow walks slowly toward Janis and Karen)

BLOODY BILL CROW: I hope all doubt as to my authenticity has been erased. For I *am* Bloody Bill Crow! *I* stole a fortune in Mexican gold. *I* hid it here, by Commanche Creek. *I* survived the Indians' lance and the hangman's noose, and now *I* have returned to claim *my* treasure!

(SOUND: Indian drums, louder than before.)

BLOODY BILL CROW: Hush!

(SOUND: a coyote howl.)

BLOODY BILL CROW: *(brandishes knife in air)* My curse upon you, Many Scalps! *(dashes offstage left)*

KAREN: I don't know about you, cousin, but I'm not waiting for Many Scalps to show up!

(Janis and Karen dash offstage right; LIGHTS OUT BRIEFLY; DRUMS FADE OUT; SPOTLIGHT ON Janis and Karen at down right.)

JANIS: Phillip! Where are you?
KAREN: Are you sure we came through this passage?
JANIS: I'm positive. Phillip!
PHILLIP: Help!

(LIGHTS UP CENTER; Phillip sits in front of rock at mid center,

hands tied behind his back with rope; Janis and Karen untie him.)

KAREN: I *told* you to be careful!

PHILLIP: Well, *I* told us to not come here! That old guy is a nut-case! He would have killed me except for his daughter.

KAREN: The rodeo queen?

PHILLIP: Her name is Maggie, and I owe her my life. Please don't make fun of her wardrobe!

JANIS: Did he find the gold?

PHILLIP: What?

JANIS: Did — he — find — the — gold?

PHILLIP: How do I know? I've been playing luggage claim for the last hour! I told him the poem you found in the book, then he went bonkers and tied me up.

JANIS: He found the gold! Come on!

(Janis races offstage left; Karen and Phillip reluctantly follow. LIGHTS OUT BRIEFLY; LIGHTS UP FULL; Bonaparte Phelps is at down right digging with a shovel.)

BONAPARTE PHELPS: *(stops digging and looks at audience)* "Would you like another railroad for supper, Senator Phelps?" Oh, I do like the sound of that! *(starts digging, then stops)* "President Phelps" sounds even better! *(resumes digging)*

(Janis, Karen and Phillip rise from behind rock at mid center.)

JANIS: Karen, what time is it?

KAREN: About five minutes past midnight.

JANIS: "The dark noon hour." Look at the shadow above where Phelps is digging.

KAREN: I don't see anything but a shadow.

PHILLIP: I do. It's a shape...like a big bird claw! The third line of the poem — "Where shaded by the eagle's claw"!

JANIS: At midnight the moonlight shines off the creek onto the wall. The shadow it forms marks the treasure spot.

KAREN: Are you sure?

BONAPARTE PHELPS: *(drops shovel)* Great thundering cockle-berries! I've never seen so much gold in my life! *(kneels and reaches into hole)*

JANIS: I'm sure.

BONAPARTE PHELPS: And it's mine! All mine!

BLOODY BILL CROW: *(o.s. left)* Now that would be dangerously presumptuous, my good sir.

(Startled, Phelps falls on his backside; Crow enters pointing a pistol at him and strolls to center stage.)

BONAPARTE PHELPS: What are you doing here?

BLOODY BILL CROW: Watching you retrieve my gold, of course. Oh, but you meant what am I doing here after you betrayed me and sent a posse on my trail? The answer to that is, I have come to exact my revenge!

(Maggie enters from left.)

MAGGIE: Please, Bill! Don't hurt him! He's an old man!

BLOODY BILL CROW: He's an old scalawag! Maggie, dearest, run along ahead, and I'll catch up. We'll take the morning train to St. Louis and spend the rest of our lives spending gold.

(Maggie comes closer to Crow; Phelps slowly rises and reaches toward his back pocket.)

MAGGIE: Bill, please! Let him go!

BLOODY BILL CROW: Maggie, stay out of this. Run along now. *(to Phelps)* Don't you move!

(SOUND: Indian drums, very louder.)

MAGGIE: Bill, please!

BLOODY BILL CROW: Maggie, stay back!

(Phelps pulls a pistol from his pocket; Crow turns to shoot him; Maggie lunges and grabs for his gun.)

MAGGIE: Don't shoot!

(SOUND: a gun shot. Phelps fires and hits Maggie, who falls dead on ground.)

BLOODY BILL CROW: Traitor!

(SOUND: a gun shot. Crow fires and hits Phelps, who falls dead on ground. Two Commanches, armed with tomahawk

and spear, appear at down left and stare at Crow, who backs away and fires at them, though they are not hit. SOUND: several gun shots.)

BLOODY BILL CROW: You won't get me this time, Many Scalps!

(Crow races offstage right.)

BLOODY BILL CROW: *(o.s. right, screams as if falling)* Aaaaaaaaa!
JANIS: Now we know where the abandoned mine shaft is.

(LIGHTS OUT BRIEFLY; DRUMS STOP. LIGHTS UP RIGHT on Janis sitting on rock at down right, Karen and Phillip standing next to her.)

PHILLIP: I still don't understand where the gold went. The old man found it, didn't he?
KAREN: But when we looked, it wasn't there. There wasn't even a hole. Or a shovel.
PHILLIP: Do you think the Indians took it? And buried the bodies? *(pause)* Am I still the only one who saw the Indians?
KAREN: What I can't figure out is who did the underlining in Janis' book? And how would they know?
JANIS: *(pause)* I'd like to have an honesty minute here. And I hope nobody gets mad.
PHILLIP: I'm nearly dead, how can I have energy left to be mad?
JANIS: Okay. I made it up. I made the whole thing up.
PHILLIP: The story about Confederates being ambushed?
JANIS: All of it.
KAREN: The tale of Bloody Bill Crow and the outlaw gang?
JANIS: All of it.
PHILLIP: And the poem?
JANIS: Especially the poem. I was reading a book about the Old West, and I just got excited.
KAREN: But what about everything we saw? What about Phillip getting tied up? You *were* tied up, weren't you, Phillip?
PHILLIP: I *think* so. Or maybe…I don't know. Maybe we all just let our imaginations run away with us. We sure didn't find any gold, and that's for sure!
KAREN: See you at school Monday.
PHILLIP: Yeh, later.

JANIS: Bye.

(Karen and Phillip exit right.)

JANIS: *(to audience)* We never said anything to anybody about what happened that night. We never went back to the cabin on Commanche Creek, either. Annnnnd, I guess maybe my honesty minute didn't last a full sixty seconds. *(stands)* When Karen and Phillip ran out of the cave, I wasn't right behind them. I heard a noise and looked back and well — something on the floor caught my eye. *(draws a Mexican gold peso from her pocket)* It doesn't look like a carrot flower. But I suppose they made them differently back in 1865. *(flips peso into the audience)*

(SOUND: Indian drums, moderate. LIGHTS OUT. DRUMS FADE OUT.)

THE END

ROCKY MOUNTAIN RENDEZVOUS

Even before Lewis and Clark's expedition of 1805–06, a few hardy men wandered the Great Plains and Rocky Mountains to hunt animals such as beaver and buffalo for their fur and hides, trading them to clothesmakers back East and abroad. The heyday of these "mountain men" was from 1800–40, and they played a large role in exploring the West. Life as a trapper was very lonely, so the mountain men would meet once a year at an annual convention or "rendezvous." A rendezvous was like a rowdy county fair, where the trappers sold their pelts and bought supplies for their next hunting trip, all the while enjoying a wide variety of entertainment — horse racing, dancing, gambling and conversing and competing in sporting events with friendly Native Americans. After the trapping business died out in the 1840s, the remaining mountain men continued to wander the West as scouts and explorers. Jim Beckwourth (1798–1866) was one-quarter Negro, one-quarter Indian and one-half European and was born in Fredericksburg, Virginia; he began trapping in 1825, lived among the Crow Indians and prospected for gold in California and Colorado. Antoine Robidou was born in St. Louis, Missouri, and began trapping in 1823; in the 1830s he became first alcalde of Sante Fe and served as a U.S. Army scout in the Mexican War. Joe Meek (1810–1875) was born in Washington County, Virginia, and began trapping in 1829. He later became the first U.S. marshal of Oregon Territory. Horse Creek, the site of the last rendezvous, was a trading center for Native Americans before Columbus.

TIME: 1839, The Last Rendezvous

PLACE: A trapper's lodge, Horse Creek, Wyoming

RUNNING TIME: 30 minutes

CAST: 21 actors, min. 7 boys, 3 girls

Joe Meek	Jim Beckwourth
Antoine Robidou	Rev. Thomas Pettigrew
Iktomi the Spider	Iktomi the Fox
3 Ducks	Spotted Elk
Spotted Elk's Husband	Rude Hunter
Kind Hunter	4 Black Bears
Sasquatch	Pine Leaf
Pine Leaf's Mother	Pine Leaf's Father

STAGE SET: four short logs placed along ground at down right as if around a campfire; a scrim or blanket painted with Native American images or signs at mid center

PROPS: Bible, 2 jugs, sack, blanket, pipe, tomahawk, 2 dead deer bodies, piece of dried meat, rope snare on a stick, snake, flowers, 2 meat slabs, short coffee table or tray, 3 bowls, wolf tooth

EFFECTS: Sound — loud whoops of merrymaking, a few gunshots and old-time fiddle music (*Little Brown Jug*)

MUSIC: *Little Brown Jug, River Duck Song, La Valse à Grand-Amour, Black Bear Curing Song, Old Rosin the Beau, Sasquatch Song*

COSTUMES: Rev. Pettigrew wears an early 19th-century Protestant minister's black shirt, black pants and white minister's collar, perhaps a crucifix around his neck. Meek, Beckwourth and Robidou dress as mountain men — light linen shirt and buckskin breeches held up by a wide leather belt, a large low-brimmed beaver hat adorned with feathers and beads or Indian designs, perhaps a fringed vest, brown moccasins; Bears, Fox, Spider, Ducks wear animal masks and appropriate coverings/markings; Pine Leaf and her Family, Spotted Elk and Husband and Rude and Kind Hunters dress as period Native Americans; Sasquatch can be garbed as a combination Yeti and Swamp Thing

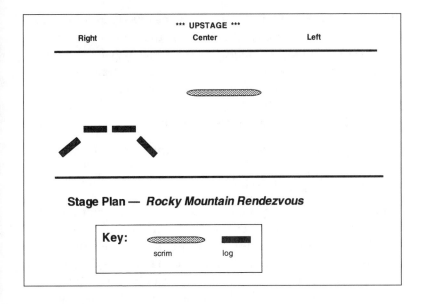

*** UPSTAGE ***

Right   Center   Left

Stage Plan — *Rocky Mountain Rendezvous*

Key: scrim   log

(LIGHTS UP RIGHT on REVEREND THOMAS PETTIGREW, a missionary on his first trip West, sitting down right on a log before a campfire and reading the Bible.)

REV. PETTIGREW: Thus saith the Lord God to Isaiah, "I am laying in Zion a foundation stone, a tested stone, a sure foundation..."

(SOUND: loud whoops of merrymaking, a few gunshots and old-time fiddle music ["Little Brown Jug"] sound offstage, startling Rev. Pettigrew. The mountain man JOE MEEK enters from left, laughing and toting a jug. He stops at center stage and breaks out into song as Rev. Pettigrew jumps up in alarm. MUSIC: "Little Brown Jug." SOUNDS FADE OUT.)

JOE MEEK *(SINGS)*
     Ha-ha-ha, it's you and me
     Little brown jug don't I love thee?

JOE MEEK: Hoooo-wee! What a glorious night for a spate of fiddle and dance! *(shuffles a quick jig step)* My apologies, Reverend. I'm Joe Meek, trapper with the Rocky Mountain Fur Company. *(shakes hands with Rev. Pettigrew)*

REV. PETTIGREW: I am Reverend Thomas Pettigrew of the Troy Missionary Conference, New York. Is this your lodge, sir?

JOE MEEK: My lodge? *(laughs heartily)* Haw-haw-haw! Why, it's anybody's who wants it, I reckon! It wasn't here a week ago, and it won't be standing a week from now. This your first rendezvous, Reverend?

REV. PETTIGREW: I must concede that it is.

(SOUND: a gunshot and an answering whoop offstage.)

REV. PETTIGREW: Is a rendezvous always such an...exuberant affair?

JOE MEEK: Reverend, these mountain men have been trapping in the wilderness for eleven months, seeing nary a human being the whole time. Rendezvous is where they sell their pelts, chew the fat and let the civilized world know they're still alive. Then, after all the fun's over, they head back into the mountains to hunt beaver...and try to stay alive till rendezvous next year. Where are you headed from here?

REV. PETTIGREW: I am on a missionary expedition to the Oregon Territory tribes — bringing the Word of God to the Cayuse and the Nez Percé.

JOE MEEK: Well, that Bible talk won't help you much with them. You have to tell the story of God and Jesus and all in language they understand. Savvy?

REV. PETTIGREW: I have extensive seminary training in the Old and New Testament, if that's what you mean.

JOE MEEK: *(shakes his head "no")* Indians already believe in God, Reverend. Why, Indians are the biggest believers in heaven and spirits and the powerful work of the Almighty you ever did see! They just believe in God a little bit differently than you or me. Now, if you're a-going to preach to Indians, you're a-going to have to see the world the way they do — or they won't listen to any of those fancy seminary words. Pull up a log and let me tell you a tale I heard at the very first rendezvous up at Green River back in '25.

(Rev. Pettigrew and Joe Meek sit down; LIGHTS FADE DOWN RIGHT, LIGHTS FADE UP LEFT AND CENTER as IKTOMI

THE SPIDER enters from left, swaggering and flailing his arms in the air as he crosses to down center.)

JOE MEEK: The Sioux tell a story about Iktomi the Spider. Iktomi is the greatest trickster in the world, you know. He can make himself into any creature or shape he likes. One morning Iktomi went to the river for a drink. Downstream a ways, he noticed a flock of ducks swimming without a care in the world and singing their happy little duck song.

(THREE DUCKS enter from left and splash about at down left; they face audience and sing. MUSIC: "River Duck Song.")

THREE DUCKS *(SING)*
Throughout the world
Who is there like me?
Who is like little me?
I can touch the sky!
I can touch the sky!
River ducks touch the sky!

(Three Ducks squat at down left and lower heads as if sleeping.)

IKTOMI THE SPIDER: Ooo, are those ducks? Yummy-yummy ducks! Lovvvvve those tender, tasty ducks! And just in time for breakfast. Let's see, what kind of animal is good for catching ducks. Weasel? No. Antelope? No. I've got it — a fox! I'll just change myself into a fox...and catch some ducks.

(Iktomi the Spider dashes behind scrim at mid center and reappears on the other side as IKTOMI THE FOX, advancing stealthily to down center where he stops and hails the Three Ducks and motions them over.)

IKTOMI THE FOX: Hellooooo, river ducks! It's Fox! I want to show you something. Swim a little closer to shore and have a talk with your old friend, Fox.
DUCK #1: Look, it's Fox. What is he doing here?
DUCK #2: *(peers closely at Iktomi)* It isn't Fox. It's Iktomi the Spider pretending to be Fox.
DUCK #1: Oh. Why would he do a thing like that?
DUCK #3: Because he wants to eat us, silly! *(shouts to Iktomi)* But

we are very intelligent river ducks. We will not be fooled by a dumb trick like that!

(Three Ducks laugh.)

IKTOMI THE FOX: *(moves back to scrim)* Darn, darn, darn! You ducks are too smart for me! I guess I'll just have to go hungry today! *(goes behind scrim)*

DUCK #1: Did you hear that? Iktomi is the cleverest animal in the world, and *we* outsmarted him!

DUCK #2: Well, after all, we *are* river ducks!

DUCK #3: River ducks touch the sky!

(Three Ducks cheer and sing last line of "River Duck Song.")

THREE DUCKS *(SING)*
River ducks touch the sky!
River ducks touch the sky!
River ducks touch the sky!

JOE MEEK: But Iktomi listened to the ducks bragging and over-heard every word they said. "Oh, these ducks are so easy to flatter," he thought. Then he changed into his spider shape again and went back to the river.

(Iktomi the Spider comes out from behind scrim and goes to down center.)

IKTOMI THE SPIDER: You ducks are sooooo smart. You have seen through my cleverest trick, so I'll just leave and wish you well.

(Three Ducks laugh.)

IKTOMI THE SPIDER: But before I leave, I feel it's my duty as a fellow river creature to warn you about the water. *(turns toward right and starts slowly toward exit)*

DUCK #1: Water? What did he say about the water?

DUCK #2: Is there something wrong with the water?

DUCK #3: Iktomi, wait! What is wrong with the water?

(Iktomi stops and turns back to the Three Ducks.)

IKTOMI THE SPIDER: *(looks skyward)* The sun.

DUCK #1: The sun? I thought he said water.

DUCK #2: The sun is wrong with the water?

DUCK #1: Or is the water wrong with the sun?

DUCK #3: Iktomi, wait! What is wrong with the water?

IKTOMI THE SPIDER: The sun shines on the water and makes a bright reflection. If you look at the water while you swim, your eyes will turn red.

THREE DUCKS: No!

IKTOMI THE SPIDER: This happened to a bunch of river ducks I know.

THREE DUCKS: It could happen to us!

IKTOMI THE SPIDER: Their eyes were very, very red. It was terrible.

THREE DUCKS: Terrible!

IKTOMI THE SPIDER: Terrible. Fortunately, I know how to prevent this terrible thing from happening.

(Iktomi turns away again and begins moving slowly to exit right; the Three Ducks flap wildly.)

THREE DUCKS: Wait! Please tell us how to keep our eyes from turning red! Please!

IKTOMI THE SPIDER: *(stops, turns to Ducks)* Well, all right. But only because you ducks are my good friends. And if I tell you what to do, you better take my advice. I don't like wasting words, you know.

DUCK #1: Yes, yes, Iktomi, anything you say!

DUCK #2 : We will take your advice!

DUCK #3: Iktomi is our good friend!

IKTOMI THE SPIDER: Very well. You must close your eyes very tightly, then the sun will not turn your eyes red.

DUCK #1: But sitting on the river all day with our eyes closed? That's boring!

DUCK #2 : Boring!

DUCK #3: Boring!

IKTOMI THE SPIDER: Then why don't you dance? Dancing with your eyes closed is a wonderful way to spend the day! Since I am your friend, I will sing a song for your dance.

DUCK #1: It *is* wonderful!

DUCK #2 : We can dance all day!

DUCK #3: Sing for us, Iktomi!

(The Three Ducks rise and dance, eyes closed. Iktomi goes to scrim, reaches behind it and pulls out a big sack. He fluffs open the sack and sings, as the Three Ducks dance nearer to him. MUSIC: "River Duck Song.")

IKTOMI THE SPIDER: *(SINGS)*
Throughout the world
Who is there like me?
Who is like little me?
I can eat the duck!
I can eat the duck!
River ducks taste so good!
DUCK #1: I love dancing on the water! This is so much fun!

(Iktomi grabs Duck #1 and stuffs it into his sack — behind the scrim.)

IKTOMI THE SPIDER: So *much* fun! Close your eyes, little ducks, and keep dancing! *(loudly hums the "River Duck Song")*
DUCK #2: To dance is divine!

(Iktomi grabs Duck #2 and stuffs it into his sack.)

IKTOMI THE SPIDER: To eat is diviner!
DUCK #2: Aaaaaaaiii! Helllllllllp!

(Duck #3 opens eyes and sees Duck #2 get stuffed into sack.)

DUCK #3: Oh no! We've been tricked! Run, everyone! Run from Iktomi the Trickster! *(dashes offstage left)*

(Iktomi hoists sack over his shoulder and goes to exit right)

IKTOMI THE SPIDER: Two out of three's not bad! *(exits)*

(LIGHTS UP RIGHT on Joe Meek and Rev. Pettigrew.)

REV. PETTIGREW: I suppose that explains to the Sioux why ducks and waterfowl are so hard to catch?
JOE MEEK: That's just part of it, Reverend. You see, when you come calling on the Indians, telling them how you're the friend and can save their souls from sin, they'll be thinking about Iktomi the Spider telling the ducks how to save their eyes from getting red.

(A loud voice — that of mountain man ANTOINE ROBIDOU — sings from offstage right. MUSIC: "La Valse à Grand-Amour.")

ANTOINE ROBIDOU: *(SINGS, o.s.)*
Allez, on danse là
Allez, on danse là
Allez, on danse là, chère!
Allez, on danse là
Allez, on danse là
Mais on danse la valse à Grand-Amour!

(Antoine Robidou enters from right and, with arms out-stretched, excitedly hails Joe Meek and Rev. Pettigrew.)

ANTOINE ROBIDOU: *Laissez les bons temps rouler!* Let the good times roll!

JOE MEEK: Antoine Robidou, you old caribou carcass! This here is Reverend Pettigrew, a soul trapper from back in the States.

REV. PETTIGREW: *(shakes hands with Robidou)* Pleased to meet you, sir.

ANTOINE ROBIDOU: *Enchanté, monsieur.*

JOE MEEK: Antoine is an engagé for Kit Carson. Heard you fellas had your best trapping season ever.

ANTOINE ROBIDOU: Ha! Not me, monsieur! *Je suis fauché!* I am broke! And I owe Jim Bridger one hundred dollars for a new saddle!

JOE MEEK: Jim Bridger! Why, I haven't seen that rascal since the rendezvous in Taos. Reverend, this Jim Bridger is the king of all the mountain men. Why, he walked around for three years with a Blackfoot arrowhead in him afore he found a sawbones to dig it out — three inches of solid iron right smack in the middle of his back. Doc said, "Jim, I am surprised this wound didn't putrefy." Bridger said, "Doc, in the mountains, meat doesn't spoil."

(Meek and Robidou laugh heartily.)

ANTOINE ROBIDOU: Sit down, and I tell you a tale I heard from Jim Bridger. He heard it from the Minnetaree, who live up on the Missouri in Dakota Territory.

(Rev. Pettigrew, Meek and Robidou sit down; LIGHTS FADE DOWN RIGHT, LIGHTS FADE UP LEFT AND CENTER on Spotted Elk sitting cross-legged at down left, sewing a blanket.)

ANTOINE ROBIDOU: A long time ago there was a woman named Spotted Elk. Her husband had got very angry one day and broke a sacred pipe over his leg. Right after that, his leg swelled up, and he got real sick. They tried every kind of magic they knew to cure it, but nothing would work.

(SPOTTED ELK'S HUSBAND enters from left, angry; he shakes the pipe and breaks it over his leg, immediately swooning and collapsing at down left; SPOTTED ELK comforts him, putting the blanket under his head.)

ANTOINE ROBIDOU: Well, after awhile, Spotted Elk, she has to go out to hunt food.

(Spotted Elk takes tomahawk from her Husband's belt and moves stealthily up left in search of game; RUDE HUNTER, dragging a dead deer, enters from left and crosses to down center.)

ANTOINE ROBIDOU: Many miles from her home, she sees a man who had just killed a big deer. She asks him for *un tout petit peu* — a very little bit. But the man is very rude. He threatens her and runs away with the deer.

(Rude Hunter threatens Spotted Elk with rude gestures, drags deer offstage right. Spotted Elk wanders up right then turns and sees KIND HUNTER enter from up left, dragging a dead deer.)

ANTOINE ROBIDOU: She goes on a bit farther and sees another man who has also killed a deer. This hunter, however, is kind and gives her some meat before leaving.

(Kind Hunter gives Spotted Elk a piece of meat, then exits right.)

ANTOINE ROBIDOU: "Cette viande est bonne! This meat is good!" says Spotted Elk, and she decides to follow the Kind Hunter through the forest.

(Spotted Elk moves around stage, crouched, peering around her, finally stopping in front of scrim at mid center.)

ANTOINE ROBIDOU: Finally, she comes to a big hunting lodge. She hears a lot of voices talking inside...talking in Black Bear language. She is very surprised when a voice from inside calls out to her:

BLACK BEAR: Come in to our lodge, Spotted Elk. We have been awaiting your arrival.

(Spotted Elk looks behind the scrim, then backs quickly away as FOUR BLACK BEARS come out from behind the scrim and stand in front of it, facing the audience in a line with Spotted Elk to their left.)

ANTOINE ROBIDOU: There were two groups of black bears. The bears on the left were *très brusque* — very rude — just like the Rude Hunter she had met in the forest.

(Black Bears #1 and #2 make rude faces, stick fingers up their nose, stick out their tongues, etc.)

ANTOINE ROBIDOU: But the bears on the right were kind, just like the Kind Hunter who gave her the good deer meat.

(Black Bears #3 and #4 shush the rude bears and bow and gently pat Spotted Elk's hands.)

BLACK BEAR #3: Spotted Elk, your husband is in truth a Black Bear. He is our son and brother.

BLACK BEAR #4: We have heard our son is in great illness. We have called you here to cure him.

BLACK BEAR #1: We are going to teach you sacred songs and dances to cure him.

BLACK BEAR #2: And you better learn them right, *ma chère belle!* Or us rude bears will eat you alllllll up! *Allez, on danse!*

(The Black Bears begin stomping their feet in rhythm to the song as Spotted Elk kneels in front of them, facing audience, and receiving the sacred curing knowledge imparted by the song. MUSIC: "Black Bear Curing Song.")

BLACK BEARS #1 & 2 *(SING)*
>Your heart is good
>Think of goodness in your dream
>Sing of goodness in your song

BLACK BEARS #3 & 4 *(SING)*
>We are black bears
>We will ask for goodness
>To visit you and stay long

(Black Bears exit behind scrim; LIGHTS OUT CENTER; Spotted Elk rises and goes down left, kneeling next to her Husband.)

ANTOINE ROBIDOU: Spotted Elk learned many sacred curing songs from the Black Bears. When she got back home, she went to her Husband and began the curing ceremony.

(Spotted Elk takes a piece of dried meat and a rope snare on a stick from her belt. She begins slowly waving the meat over her Husband's injured leg and humming the melody to"Black Bear Curing Song.")

ANTOINE ROBIDOU: The Black Bears had told her to take a small piece of dried meat and a snare...and hold the meat over her husband's leg. *Prenez garde!* Watch out!

(A snake pops out from her Husband's leg, which she catches in the snare and kills with her tomahawk.)

ANTOINE ROBIDOU: Didn't a big ugly snake head pop out of the leg trying to get the meat! But Spotted Elk caught the snake in the snare and killed it with her tomahawk. You see, *mes amis*, the snake was the cause of the illness in the leg; it was the spirit that had been offended when her husband broke the sacred pipe.

(Spotted Elk's Husband rises, cured, and embraces her happily; they exit left; LIGHTS OUT LEFT, LIGHTS UP RIGHT on Rev. Pettigrew, Joe Meek and Antoine Robidou.)

REV. PETTIGREW: I suppose that explains why the Minnetaree dance to heal leg wounds?

ANTOINE ROBIDOU: *Voilà la réponse, monsieur.* That is the answer.

JOE MEEK: But not all the answer, Reverend. You see, to the Indian, that story tells how people are connected to the world around them. Connected deep, in ways you might not savvy right off.

(A loud voice — that of mountain man JIM BECKWOURTH — sings from offstage right. MUSIC: "Old Rosin the Beau.")

JIM BECKWOURTH: *(SINGS, o.s.)*
I've traveled this country over
And now to the next I will go
For I know that good quarters await me
To welcome old Rosin the Beau

(Jim Beckwourth enters from right, toting a jug; Joe Meek picks up his jug and clinks it with Beckwourth's as Meek and Antoine Robidou sing with Beckwourth on chorus.)

JIM BECKWOURTH, JOE MEEK & ANTOINE ROBIDOU: *(SING)*
To welcome old Rosin the Beau
To welcome old Rosin the Beau
I know that good quarters await me
To welcome old Rosin the Beau

(Beckwourth, Meek and Robidou shake hands and clap shoulders.)

JOE MEEK: Jim Beckwourth, I want you to meet a good friend of ours. His name is Pettigrew — Reverend Pettigrew, to ratify the corn. And he's headed up Oregon way. Didn't you just come back from there?

JIM BECKWOURTH: Cross the Cascades almost to Canada and the Pacific, I was. It's where I come upon the Sasquatch.

REV. PETTIGREW: The what?

JIM BECKWOURTH: Sasquatch. S-A-S...Q-U-A...T-C-H, Sasquatch. Oh, it is a fearsome creature!

REV. PETTIGREW: Is it a beast? Or a man?

JIM BECKWOURTH: Neither...and both. Take a seat and pass around the jug. This here is a story liable to exfluncticate every hair on your head.

(LIGHTS FADE OUT RIGHT; STAGE STAYS BLACK.)

JIM BECKWOURTH: A long time ago, a band of Snohomish warriors got crossways with the Great Spirit…did something awful ornery to make him heap powerful mad. After they died, these warriors weren't allowed into the Happy Hunting Grounds. They had to haunt the woods where they'd lived. And the Great Spirit turned them into — Sasquatch!

(SPOTLIGHT UP CENTER on SASQUATCH standing at down center, arms upraised and snarling at the audience.)

JIM BECKWOURTH: The Sasquatch was part-ape and part-grizzly bear and still somewhat part of a man, though not much. They ate human flesh, and because they'd been fierce warriors during their human lives, they were especially dangerous.

(LIGHTS UP LEFT AND CENTER; PINE LEAF enters from left, picking flowers as she moves to down center and back to down left; she does not see Sasquatch, but Sasquatch sees her and runs back by scrim to watch her unobserved.)

JIM BECKWOURTH: One day, this particular Sasquatch was haunting the woods, when he saw a pretty Snohomish girl passing by picking flowers. Her name was Pine Leaf, and she was the daughter of the local chieftain. Well, this Sasquatch had a tender heart in him. And string me up for possum bait, if he didn't fall head over heels in love with the girl!

(Pine Leaf exits left and Sasquatch moves to down center, holding his huge furry paws against his heart.)

JIM BECKWOURTH: Course, being a Sasquatch he couldn't exactly come courting her in the usual way. So he had another idea.

(Sasquatch goes behind scrim, grabs a slab of meat and leaves it on ground at down left; he dashes back to the scrim and watches unobserved as PINE LEAF'S MOTHER enters from left and discovers the meat.)

PINE LEAF'S MOTHER: Pine Leaf!
PINE LEAF: Yes, mother, what is it?
PINE LEAF'S MOTHER: Come here and look at this meat!

(Pine Leaf enters from left and looks at the meat.)

PINE LEAF: That is meat, mother.

PINE LEAF'S MOTHER: I know it's meat, I want to know how it got here at our front door!

PINE LEAF: I have no idea! I don't even eat meat, mother! *(makes gagging sign)*

PINE LEAF'S MOTHER: I am going to call your father! Father! Come look at this meat!

(PINE LEAF'S FATHER enters from left and looks at the meat.)

PINE LEAF'S FATHER: That is meat, wife.

PINE LEAF'S MOTHER: I know it is! I want to know who put it there!

(Pine Leaf's Father bends and examines the meat, poking and sniffing it.)

PINE LEAF'S FATHER: I think it is good meat. *(sniffs)* I think it is Sasquatch meat.

PINE LEAF & PINE LEAF'S MOTHER: Sasquatch!

PINE LEAF'S FATHER: Yes. For some reason, a Sasquatch has decided to bring us meat.

PINE LEAF'S MOTHER: Well, just throw it to the dogs. We won't have any old Sasquatch bringing us his old dead meat!

PINE LEAF'S FATHER: *(picks up meat and hands it to Pine Leaf's Mother)* It is unwise to reject a gift from a spirit, especially a Sasquatch. If the meat is good, we must eat it.

(Sasquatch has crept closer to the family; Pine Leaf sees him and screams.)

PINE LEAF: Aaiiiii!

PINE LEAF'S FATHER: It is the Sasquatch! What do you want from us?

(Sasquatch says nothing but lurches and lopes and grunts around the family, peering at them, then hiding his face as if embarrassed.)

PINE LEAF: Father, the Sasquatch cannot talk in human language.

PINE LEAF'S MOTHER: *(threatens Sasquatch with the meat slab)* No, but he's a spirit, and spirits can sing! Out with it! What do you want from us?

(Sasquatch stands up straight and sings to Pine Leaf. MUSIC: "Sasquatch Song.")

SASQUATCH: *(SINGS)*
Your heart is hard against me, dear
Your heart runs cold like an icy stream
You are the flower of the forest
I see you often in my dream
I am a lonely Sasquatch
It is lonely being dead
If you were my wife, dearest Pine Leaf
I would be so very happy instead
But I would still, of course, be dead

(Sasquatch kneels on one knee before Pine Leaf, hands folded, head bowed; Pine Leaf turns to her parents.)

PINE LEAF: Oh, no! The Sasquatch wants to marry me!

PINE LEAF'S FATHER: It is bad medicine to reject a request from a spirit, especially after he has given us a gift.

PINE LEAF'S MOTHER: Well, I am not going to have my daughter marry something like that!

PINE LEAF: Think of something, father. Please!

PINE LEAF'S FATHER: *(approaches Sasquatch)* O, mighty Sasquatch, we thank you for your interest in our family — especially our daughter.

PINE LEAF: Father!

(Sasquatch raises head and grunts expectantly.)

PINE LEAF'S FATHER: But I cannot let her go to you—

(Sasquatch grunts angrily.)

PINE LEAF'S FATHER: Or any other suitor — without first putting you to a test of skill and intelligence.

(Sasquatch nods head "yes"and grunts vigorously.)

PINE LEAF'S FATHER: The test I choose is the Wolf Tooth Game.

(Pine Leaf's Father and Sasquatch sit down cross-legged facing each other as Pine Leaf brings out from left wing a short coffee table or tray and sets it between her Father and

Sasquatch; Pine Leaf's Mother sets three small bowls on table.)

PINE LEAF'S FATHER: Under one of these bowls is the Wolf Tooth. *(begins moving bowls around as Sasquatch nods agreement)* I move the bowls. When I stop, you must find the Wolf Tooth.

(Pine Leaf's Father stops the bowls; Sasquatch points to one; Father lifts up bowl, but it does not have the Wolf Tooth.)

PINE LEAF'S FATHER: Aha! You did not find the Wolf Tooth. Game over, you lose. No daughter for you.

(Sasquatch roars and raises fist as if to hammer Pine Leaf's Father in head.)

PINE LEAF'S FATHER: All right, all right! Two out of three, whatever you say.

(Pine Leaf's Father moves bowls around; stops moving them; Sasquatch chooses and uncovers the Wolf Tooth; Sasquatch jumps up and dances with glee as Pine Leaf moans.)

SASQUATCH: Rrrrrrrrowwwwwr!

PINE LEAF: Motherrrrrr! Fatherrrrr!

PINE LEAF'S MOTHER: *(slaps Sasquatch with the meat slab)* Sit down, you monster! You must win two games out of three before you get our daughter. And if you lose this time, you must go away and leave us alone.

(Sasquatch grunts assent and sits down; Pine Leaf's Father moves bowls around; stops moving them; starts them again; stops them; starts them; stops them; starts them; Sasquatch roars in frustration.)

SASQUATCH: Rrrrrrrrowwwwwr!

PINE LEAF'S MOTHER: Enough already, let the poor monster make his choice!

(Sasquatch hesitates, starts to choose first bowl, stops and chooses second instead, then raises finger from that bowl and grunts knowingly.)

SASQUATCH: Rrrrrrow-ow-ow-ow-owwwr!

(Sasquatch picks up third bowl; the Wolf Tooth is not under it.)

PINE LEAF'S FATHER: No Wolf Tooth! Game over! You lose!

(Sasquatch hangs head silently and rises, slowly moving to scrim; Pine Leaf's Father carries off the table and exits left, followed by Pine Leaf's Mother who drags Pine Leaf offstage left as she waves goodbye to Sasquatch exiting behind scrim; LIGHTS FADE OUT LEFT AND CENTER, LIGHTS UP RIGHT on Rev. Pettigrew, Joe Meek, Antoine Robidou and Jim Beckwourth.)

JIM BECKWOURTH: Now, by the horn spoon, fellers, that story is true as me sitting here! And what's more, even though Pine Leaf had given him the mitten, that lovesick Sasquatch kept bringing the family meat for years and years.

(Beckwourth, Meek and Robidou laugh heartily.)

REV. PETTIGREW: Surely, gentlemen, you don't believe that wild tale is true?

JOE MEEK: It doesn't matter if *we* think it's true, Reverend. The Indians believe it is.

ANTOINE ROBIDOU: And if you think, like the Sasquatch did, that you can conquer the Indian's heart and mind by scaring him — or by throwing little presents at him — you will fail, *mon ami*. Every time!

REV. PETTIGREW: Hmmm. *(ponders a moment)* Instead of fighting a bigger adversary with his weapons, you should find a way to compete using your strength. *(brandishes the Bible)* Why, it's like the story of David and Goliath in the Bible!

JIM BECKWOURTH: *(chuckles)* Heh-heh-heh. Not bad for a tenderfoot. *(shoves a jug into Rev. Pettigrew's hands)* Here, have some Rocky Mountain Apple Brandy! It'll keep you warm from here to Oregon!

(Beckwourth begins singing and others join in. MUSIC: "Little Brown Jug.")

MEEK, ROBIDOU, BECKWOURTH & REV. PETTIGREW: *(SING)*
Ha-ha-ha, it's you and me
Little brown jug don't I love thee?

Ha-ha-ha, can't you see
Little brown jug that I love thee?

(LIGHTS OUT.)

THE END

Little Brown Jug
(traditional, arranged by L.E. McCullough)

Ha- ha- ha, it's you and me; lit- tle brown jug, don't I love thee?

Ha- ha- ha, can't you see, lit- tle brown jug, that I love thee!

River Duck Song
(words & music: L.E. McCullough)

Through- out the world who is there like me? Who is

like lit- tle me? I can touch the sky! I can touch the sky!

Ri- ver ducks touch the sky!

© L.E. McCullough 1997

La Valse à Grand-Amour
(words & music by Serge Lainé, arr. by L.E. McCullough)

All- ez, on danse là; all- ez, on danse là; all- ez, on danse là,

chère! All- ez, on danse là; all- ez, on danse là;

mais on danse la valse à Grand- A- mour!

© Serge Lainé 1986

§ English Translation §

Let's dance; let's dance; let's dance, dear!
Let's dance; let's dance;
But let's dance that Big-Love's waltz!

Black Bear Curing Song
(words & music by L.E. McCullough)

Your heart is good; think of good-ness in your dream; sing of

good-ness in your song; We are black bears; we will ask for

good- ness to vi- sit you and stay long

© L.E. McCullough 1997

Old Rosin the Beau
(traditional, arranged by L.E. McCullough)

Sasquatch Song
(words & music: L.E. McCullough)

Your heart is hard a- gainst me, dear, your

heart runs cold like an i- cy stream. You are the flo- wer of the

for- est, I see you of- ten in my dream. I

am — a lone- ly Sas- quatch; it is lone- ly be- ing

dead If you were my wife, dear- est Pine Leaf I would

be so ve- ry hap-py in- stead But I would still, of course, be dead

TURQUOISE TOM, THE VERSIFYING BANDIT OF OLD CALIFORNIA

Turquoise Tom, the Versifying Bandit of Old California is based on the exploits of a highway bandit nicknamed "Black Bart," who from 1875-1883 robbed over two dozen Wells Fargo stagecoaches in northern California, occasionally leaving short poems at the scene of the crime. Newspapers of the day took great delight in embellishing his deeds, portraying him as a nattily-attired Western Robin Hood striking blows for the Little Man against Big Business. Black Bart's reign of terror ended when a handkerchief at the scene of a robbery was traced to a laundry in San Francisco and linked to a customer named Charles E. Boles, originally from Decatur, Illinois. When Boles went to prison, the stage coach robberies stopped — and so did the poems of Black Bart.

TIME: 1875-1880

PLACE: Copperopolis, California

RUNNING TIME: 20 minutes

CAST: 18 actors, min. 5 boys, 1 girl

Buckshot Bill	Pancho Pescado
Whispering Jim	Turquoise Tom/Percival the Editor
2 Stage Drivers	2 Shotgun Messengers
6 Passengers	2 Stage Horses
Sheriff	Matilda the Reporter

STAGE SET: a large boulder, 8 stools, a table

PROPS: smoking pipe, harmonica, bandana, shotgun, pistol, payroll bag, 2 long pencils, flower bouquet, several pieces of paper

EFFECTS: Sound — a trumpet bleat

MUSIC: *The Ballad of Turquoise Tom* sung and played to the air of the old cowboy song *Punchin' Dough*

COSTUMES: all characters dress in late 19th-century Western clothes as seen in typical Western movies; Sheriff has a gun holster and star badge; Horses wear horse masks and black pajamas or sweatsuits; Turquoise Tom wears turquoise or light blue-colored clothing and dresses like a flamboyant dandy in serape, stetson, ruffled shirt and tuxedo-style pants; he is loaded with turquoise jewelry, has a gun holster at his side and wears a flour sack over his head with eye, mouth and nose holes; Percival the Editor dresses as a nerd and wears a vest or suspenders, too short shirt sleeves, a pencil stuck behind his ear, eye glasses and an eye-shade visor

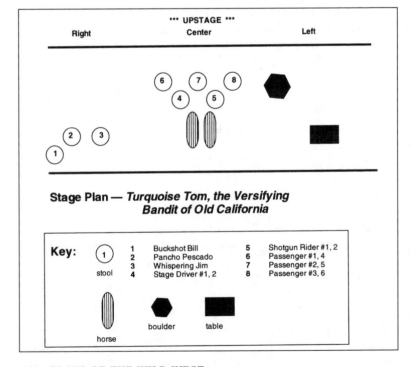

Stage Plan — *Turquoise Tom, the Versifying Bandit of Old California*

Key:

1	Buckshot Bill	5 Shotgun Rider #1, 2
2	Pancho Pescado	6 Passenger #1, 4
3	Whispering Jim	7 Passenger #2, 5
4	Stage Driver #1, 2	8 Passenger #3, 6

stool

horse   boulder   table

(LIGHTS UP STAGE RIGHT, where Three Men — BUCKSHOT BILL, PANCHO PESCADO, WHISPERING JIM — sit on stools right to left with Buckshot Bill closest to stage center. Buckshot Bill cleans out a pipe, Pancho Pescado polishes his boot toe with a bandana, Whispering Jim toots on the harmonica. Buckshot Bill stands and motions for quiet.)

BUCKSHOT BILL: Hear ye, hear ye! The official bi-weekly annual monthly meeting of the Tale Teller's Club of Copperopolis, California will now come to order. All present say, "Here!"

PANCHO PESCADO: ¡Yo estoy aqui! Pancho Pescado is here!

BUCKSHOT BILL: I, Buckshot Bill the fastest tongue in the West, is here!

(Whispering Jim whispers into Pancho's ear.)

PANCHO PESCADO: Whispering Jim says he's here!

BUCKSHOT BILL: Then why doesn't he say so, durn it?

(Pancho shrugs, Whispering Jim toots a note on the harmonica.)

BUCKSHOT BILL: Well then, who's got a tale to tell?

(Whispering Jim whispers into Pancho's ear.)

PANCHO PESCADO: Whispering Jim says he's got a tale.

BUCKSHOT BILL: About what?

(Whispering Jim whispers into Pancho's ear.)

PANCHO PESCADO: About the time the King of England came to Gizzard's Gulch.

BUCKSHOT BILL: So?

(Whispering Jim whispers into Pancho's ear.)

PANCHO PESCADO: And got chased up a tree by a bear.

BUCKSHOT BILL: And what's so extra-ordinary about that? Kings get chased up trees every day!

(Whispering Jim whispers into Pancho's ear.)

PANCHO PESCADO: In his underwear?

BUCKSHOT BILL: Oh, we've heard that a hundred times! I've got a new tale that's never been told, about the biggest stagecoach robber in the West. It's a tale full of close shaves and hot lead, blazing guns and thundering hooves, danger and poetry...

(Whispering Jim whispers into Pancho's ear.)

PANCHO PESCADO: Poetry?

BUCKSHOT BILL: That's right, you half-literate varmints — poetry! It's called "Turquoise Tom, the Versifying Bandit of Old California." Give a listen, and I'll tell it the way it was...

(LIGHTS OUT STAGE RIGHT; LIGHTS UP CENTER STAGE on the "stagecoach" drawn by TWO HORSES, kneeling and tromping their hooves in place. STAGE DRIVER #1 and SHOTGUN MESSENGER #1 sit on stools directly behind the horses; behind them are PASSENGER #1, PASSENGER #2 and PASSENGER #3 seated on higher stools and situated so that Passenger #1 flanks out to the right of Stage Driver, Passenger #3 flanks out to the left of Shotgun Messenger and Passenger #2 sits between Stage Driver and Shotgun Messenger. MUSIC: Pancho Pescado sings "The Ballad of Turquoise Tom.")

PANCHO PESCADO *(SINGS)*

Come all you young waddies, I'll sing you the song
Of a stage-robbing bandit they called Turquoise Tom
His robbing was daring, his clothes they were fine
But his poems they were simply the worst kind of crime

(five-second harmonica interlude)

BUCKSHOT BILL: On the twenty-sixth of July, 18 and 75, the Wells Fargo stage was headed out of Sonora to Milton. It was a hot summer's day, and the horses were sweating something awful.

HORSES: Neeeeiġġġhhhh! Sure is hot on this dusty trail! Neeeeiġġġhhhh! How about some coooooool water, driver? Neeeeiġġġhhhh!

BUCKSHOT BILL: The stage had just climbed to the top of a steep grade, and the tired team had slowed to a walk. It was a perfect place for an ambush, and suddenly, out stepped a man in a mask!

(TURQUOISE TOM steps out from behind boulder; underneath his serape he appears to have a pistol, which he points at Stage Driver and Shotgun Messenger.)

TURQUOISE TOM: Halt that stage, driver!

(Stage Driver struggles to rein in Horses, Horses rear and neigh, Passengers bounce in the air, Shotgun Messenger fumbles with shotgun and points butt-end toward Turquoise Tom.)

TURQUOISE TOM: Drop that shotgun, messenger!
SHOTGUN MESSENGER #1: Yessir! *(drops shotgun)*
TURQUOISE TOM: Everybody, put your hands up in the air!

(Stage Driver, Shotgun Messenger and Passengers slowly raise hands above heads. Turquoise Tom turns to Horses.)

TURQUOISE TOM: I said, *everybody!*
HORSES: Neeeeigggghhhh! *(quickly raise front hooves)*
TURQUOISE TOM: That's better. Now, hand over that payroll bag, driver!
STAGE DRIVER #1: Yessir!

(He hands payroll bag to Passenger #1, who hands it to Passenger #2, who hands it to Passenger #3, who hands it to Shotgun Messenger, who tosses it on the ground in front of Turquoise Tom.)

TURQUOISE TOM: Much obliged. *(turns to Shotgun Messenger)* Did I say you could put your hands down?
STAGE DRIVER, SHOTGUN MESSENGER & PASSENGERS: Nosir!
TURQUOISE TOM: Then put 'em up! Everybody!
SHOTGUN MESSENGER #1: Yessir!

(Stage Driver, Shotgun Messenger and Passengers raise hands.)

TURQUOISE TOM: Put 'em down!

(Stage Driver, Shotgun Messenger, Passengers and Horses lower hands.)

TURQUOISE TOM: *(paces a few steps, staring at others)* Put 'em up!

(Stage Driver, Shotgun Messenger, Passengers and Horses raise hands.)

TURQUOISE TOM: Down!

(Stage Driver, Shotgun Messenger, Passengers and Horses lower hands.)

TURQUOISE TOM: Up!

(Stage Driver, Shotgun Messenger, Passengers and Horses raise hands.)

TURQUOISE TOM: Down!

(Stage Driver, Shotgun Messenger, Passengers and Horses lower hands.)

TURQUOISE TOM: Up!

(Stage Driver, Shotgun Messenger, Passengers and Horses raise hands.)

TURQUOISE TOM: Down!

(Stage Driver, Shotgun Messenger, Passengers and Horses lower hands.)

TURQUOISE TOM: Behind your back!

(Stage Driver, Shotgun Messenger, Passengers and Horses start to raise hands, then hastily put hands behind back.)

TURQUOISE TOM: Ha! Caught you that time! Well, I'm on my way. *(picks up payroll bag and turns to exit left)* Have a nice day.

PASSENGER #3: Excuse me, Mr. Bandit.

TURQUOISE TOM: *(turns and faces Passenger #3)* You were speaking to moi?

PASSENGER #3: Yessir, Mr. Bandit, sir. We are all very excited about your robbing the stage.

PASSENGER #2: I have never been robbed by a real masked bandit!

PASSENGER #1: I can't wait to tell my friends back East all about it!

TURQUOISE TOM: *(waves pistol)* Be my guest.

PASSENGER #3: But who shall we say robbed us?

PASSENGER #2: *Whom.* It's whom, not who.

PASSENGER #1: Who, whom, whatever. We need to know your moniker.

TURQUOISE TOM: My what?

PASSENGER #3: Your handle.

PASSENGER #2: Your sobriquet.

PASSENGER #1: Your nickname.

TURQUOISE TOM: Oh, of course. *(steps forward to down center, faces audience and proclaims with pride)* They call me Turquoise Tom.

PASSENGER #3: So he dresses up in fancy duds and cheap jewelry. Some bandit!

TURQUOISE TOM: This jewelry is *not* cheap!

PASSENGER #2: A *real* bandit would leave a sign, a special calling card that identifies him each and every time he strikes!

PASSENGER #1: Like hanging a victim with a lariat drenched in blood. *(throttles Passenger #2)*

PASSENGER #3: Or branding the horses with a secret symbol.

HORSES: *(rear and shy)* Neeeeigggghhhh!

PASSENGER #2: Or shooting his name in bullet holes on the side of the stage.

TURQUOISE TOM: *(brandishes pistol)* I am a real bandit!

PASSENGER #1: Yeh, sure, prove it!

(Turquoise Tom draws a pencil and a sheet of paper from his serape, scribbles onto the paper and throws it on the ground in front of the stage; he exits left, as the Shotgun Messenger picks up the paper and reads.)

SHOTGUN MESSENGER #1:
"I've labored long and hard for bread
For riches and for money
If you who read this think I'm bad
Then you can soak your heads in honey"

STAGE DRIVER #1: This is a poem. He's written a goldurn poem.

PASSENGER #3: It's not a very good poem.

PASSENGER #2: But it is a poem.

PASSENGER #1: Whoever heard of a bandit who wrote poems?

(LIGHTS OUT CENTER STAGE, as Stage Driver #1, Shotgun

Messenger #1 and Passengers #1, 2 and 3 exit right; LIGHTS UP LEFT on the Newspaper Office where MATILDA, a Newspaper Reporter, sits on a table, writing on a sheet of paper.)

BUCKSHOT BILL: Who indeed? But it wasn't long till almost the whole high-falutin' world heard about it, thanks to an enterprising young newspaper reporter on the *Copperopolis Gazette*.

MATILDA: *(calls out toward offstage left)* Percival! Oh, Percival! *(faces audience)* Where is an editor when you need one? I've got a story that's going to be front page news on every paper in the nation!

(PERCIVAL THE EDITOR enters from stage left and stands behind the table.)

PERCIVAL: Morning, Matilda. You called?

MATILDA: *(hands him her paper)* I wrote.

PERCIVAL: *(reads from paper)* "Versifying Bandit Robs Wells Fargo Stage; Terrorizes Passengers with Pitiful Poetry." Was the poetry really that bad?

MATILDA: The driver and both horses had to be hospitalized.

PERCIVAL: That *is* pitiful poetry. Maybe he's just a beginner poet.

MATILDA: It sounds more like he's a beginner bandit. *(turns and heads offstage right)*

PERCIVAL: Ahem, well, that may be, nobody's perfect — where are you going?

MATILDA: I'm going to track down Turquoise Tom.

PERCIVAL: Wait! You can't go!

MATILDA: *(stops, turns)* Why not?

PERCIVAL: Because I was going to ask you to eat lunch with me today.

MATILDA: You should have asked yesterday. *(turns and heads offstage right)*

PERCIVAL: I did. But you said to ask you tomorrow.

MATILDA: That was yesterday. *(exits right)*

PERCIVAL: But yesterday's tomorrow is today. *(faces audience, crumples paper)* Rats! Someday, I'll win her heart! *(exits left)*

(LIGHTS OUT STAGE LEFT. MUSIC: Pancho Pescado sings "The Ballad of Turquoise Tom.")

PANCHO PESCADO *(SINGS)*
From Smartville to Quincy, he roamed and he robbed
That poem-writin' bandit they called Turquoise Tom
His deeds they were daring, his aim fast and true
But his poems just got worse, they stunk — P.U.!

(five-second harmonica interlude)

(LIGHTS UP STAGE LEFT on Turquoise Tom at down left; he faces audience and pulls out a pencil from his holster and scribbles on a piece of paper.)

BUCKSHOT BILL: As the years went by, Turquoise Tom robbed stage after stage...and wrote poem after poem. No one could catch him...not the law, not Wells Fargo...

(LIGHTS UP STAGE RIGHT on Matilda who crosses to down center, looking around with pencil and paper in hand; Turquoise Tom sneaks off right.)

BUCKSHOT BILL: Not even the reporter, Matilda, who doggedly followed his trail, writing story after story that made Turquoise Tom the best known and most feared criminal in the West.

(Matilda crosses to down left and pauses to write on the table.)

MATILDA: Percival! Oh, Percival! He's never here when I need him!

(Percival enters from stage left and stands behind the table, his hands holding a flower bouquet behind his back)

PERCIVAL: Morning, Matilda. *(presents flowers)* I was wondering if we could have lunch today—
MATILDA: *(hands him her paper, takes flowers)* Sorry, no time. It's almost tomorrow. Should have asked me yesterday. Here's the latest story on Turquoise Tom. *(hugs herself, sniffs flowers and smiles)* Ooooh, what a villain!
PERCIVAL: *(reads from paper)* "Versifying Bandit Strikes Again:

Wounds Three Deputies with Stray Rhymes." Matilda, I think you're in love with this man.

MATILDA: Don't be silly! He's an evildoer!

PERCIVAL: But you *love* his poems. I can see it in your eyes.

MATILDA: Percival, you're just jealous. *(hands back flowers)*

PERCIVAL: Well, Matilda, you're just…just…

MATILDA: *(turns and rushes offstage right)* I have to catch the noon stage to Santa Rosa. Turquoise Tom was seen nearby.

PERCIVAL: You're just…the most wonderful girl in the entire world. *(wraps paper around flowers, exits left)*

(LIGHTS OUT STAGE LEFT; LIGHTS UP CENTER STAGE on the stagecoach drawn by Two Horses, kneeling and tromping their hooves in place. STAGE DRIVER #2 and SHOTGUN MESSENGER #2 sit on stools directly behind the horses; behind them are PASSENGER #4, PASSENGER #5 and PASSENGER #6 seated on higher stools and situated so that Passenger #4 flanks out to the right of Stage Driver, Passenger #6 flanks out to the left of Shotgun Messenger and Passenger #5 sits between Stage Driver and Shotgun Messenger.)

BUCKSHOT BILL: On the twentieth of November, 18 and 80, the Wells Fargo stage was headed out of Redding to Roseburg. It was a cold winter's day, and the horses were shivering something awful.

HORSES: Neeeeiggghhhh! Sure is cold on this icy trail! Neeeeiggghhhh! How about some hot chocolate and marshmallows, driver? Neeeeiggghhhh!

BUCKSHOT BILL: The stage had just climbed to the top of a steep grade, and the tired team had slowed to a walk. It was a perfect place for an ambush, and suddenly, out stepped a man — with a pencil!

(Turquoise Tom steps out from behind boulder and levels his pencil at Stage Driver and Shotgun Messenger.)

TURQUOISE TOM: Halt that stage, driver!

PASSENGERS: Oh no, it's Turquoise Tom, the Versifying Bandit!

(Stage Driver struggles to rein in Horses, Horses rear and

neigh, Passengers bounce in the air, Shotgun Messenger fumbles with shotgun and points butt-end toward Turquoise Tom.)

TURQUOISE TOM: Drop that shotgun, messenger!

SHOTGUN MESSENGER #2: Yessir! *(drops shotgun)*

TURQUOISE TOM: Everybody, put your hands up in the air!

(Shotgun Messenger, Passengers and Horses raise hands above heads; Stage Driver grabs payroll bag and holds it aloft.)

STAGE DRIVER #2: Easy with that pencil, pard. I've got the payroll right here!

PASSENGER #4: *(holds out wallet and watch)* Take all my money and valuables. We don't want any trouble!

PASSENGER #5: And we don't want any poetry!

PASSENGER #6: Anything but the poetry! Shoot us, stab us, feed us to wolves, but please — no poetry!

TURQUOISE TOM: *(threatens Passenger #6 with pencil)* What's wrong with my poetry?

PASSENGER #6: *(shrinks back in terror)* Nothing, sir, nothing at all.

TURQUOISE TOM: It's dangerous poetry, isn't it? Bites like a bobcat. Stings like a scorpion. Poetry more deadly than a hail of bullets from a smoking six-gun. *(crouches in gunfighter stance with pencil)* Hold on, I feel a poem coming right now!

(Stage Driver, Shotgun Messenger and Passengers duck and cover their heads; Horses neigh.)

TURQUOISE TOM: *(straightens, puts pencil back in holster)* Just kidding. Now, hand over your valuables.

(As Passengers, Stage Driver and Shotgun Messenger reach into their pockets, Matilda enters from right with the SHERIFF behind her and approaches center stage.)

MATILDA: Sheriff, look! It's Turquoise Tom, and he's robbing that stage!

TURQUOISE TOM: *(turns and sees Matilda)* Matilda!

SHERIFF: *(draws pistol, points it at Turquoise Tom)* Drop that pencil, Tom, or I'll fill you full of lead!

TURQUOISE TOM: *(draws pencil, points it at Sheriff)* Drop that pistol, Sheriff, or I'll fill you full of poetry!

(Sheriff puts his pistol back in holster; Matilda rushes to Turquoise Tom.)

TURQUOISE TOM: Stand back, Miss; this pencil means business.

MATILDA: I can see by the notches in the barrel. Would you write a poem for me?

TURQUOISE TOM: You? You like my poems?

MATILDA: They're so...unique. I've never read anything...quite like them.

TURQUOISE TOM: *(moves closer to her)* They don't frighten you?

MATILDA: Not a bit. In fact, I think they're...to die for. *(points to his pencil)* But as long as you live by the pencil, Tom, we'll always be apart.

TURQUOISE TOM: I have no other choice, Matilda. I'm an outlaw poet.

MATILDA: Hang up your pencil, Tom. If you love me, hang it up, and promise you'll never write again!

(Turquoise Tom looks at pencil, then at Matilda, then at pencil.)

MATILDA: *(kneels)* Please, Tom, no more poetry!

TURQUOISE TOM: I promise!

(Turquoise Tom drops pencil and embraces Matilda; Sheriff draws his pistol and rushes over.)

SHERIFF: Hands up, Tom! You're under arrest!

(Stage Driver, Shotgun Messenger and Passengers gather around Tom, pulling him away from Matilda.)

PASSENGER #4: Take off his mask!

(Passenger #5 takes off Tom's mask; all gasp when they see it is Percival.)

MATILDA: Percival!

PASSENGER #5: Why, it's the editor of the Gazette!

PASSENGER #6: How'd he get in there?

PERCIVAL: I did it all for you, Matilda.

MATILDA: For me?

PERCIVAL: Even though I saw you every day at the newspaper, you never had time for me. You were always off chasing one story or another. I decided that if *I* were a story, you might chase me.

MATILDA: Oh, Tom! I mean, Percival!

(Sheriff prods Tom offstage left.)

PERCIVAL: We'll have lots of time for lunch now...if you enjoy prison food. *(exits)*

MATILDA: *(waves farewell, sighs sadly)* Ask me yesterday.

(LIGHTS OUT STAGE CENTER; LIGHTS UP STAGE RIGHT where Buckshot Bill, Pancho Pescado and Whispering Jim sit on stools.)

BUCKSHOT BILL: And so, amigos, that is the true tale of Turquoise Tom, the Versifying Bandit of Old California. A desperate character, indeed.

(Whispering Jim whispers into Pancho's ear.)

BUCKSHOT BILL: What's he want now?

PANCHO PESCADO: Whispering Jim wants to know if Tom ever got out of prison.

BUCKSHOT BILL: Somebody from the outside — a woman they say — smuggled him a pencil stub, and he managed to write a limerick that knocked out the guard. He was never seen again in these parts. But about ten years later, down in Mexico, there came word of a strange hombre who held up trains...with the worst goldang trumpet playing you ever heard!

(SOUND CUE: Trumpet bleat offstage. LIGHTS OUT THEN UP FULL on entire cast at center stage. MUSIC: "The Ballad of Turquoise Tom.")

ENTIRE CAST *(SINGS)*
Now that is the story of old Turquoise Tom
Whose love for Matilda was ever so strong
His robbing was daring, his clothes they were fine
But his poems they were simply the worst kind of crime

(LIGHTS OUT.)

THE END

The Ballad of Turquoise Tom
(music: traditional, words: L.E. McCullough)

Come all you young wad- dies I'll sing you a

song Of a stage- rob- bing ban- dit they called Tur- quoise

Tom His rob- bing was dar- ing, his clothes they were

fine But his poems they were sim- ply the worst kind of

crime

words © L.E. McCullough 1997

VINEGAR PETE'S CALICO WHISKER PIE

One of the most enduring images of the Wild West is the chuck wagon cook, or "cookie," as the man who prepared meals for the cowboys was commonly called. In addition to managing the food supplies on the long cattle drives and around the ranch house, chuck wagon cooks also frequently performed services as barber, doctor, dentist, banker, referee in disputes and stakeholder in bets, and maybe even entertained the outfit with some musical renditions. Cooks had the reputation of being eccentric and sometimes surly; the saying among cowboys was that "only a fool argues with a skunk, a mule or a cook." Yet, a good cook was essential for a successful cattle drive. "Chuck," incidentally, was the cowboy's term for "food."

TIME: 1879

PLACE: On the Spring roundup trail

RUNNING TIME: 20 minutes

CAST: 17 actors, min. 7 boys, 5 girls

Vinegar Pete Flynn	Matilda, a Calico Cat
Black Jack Rafferty	Haywire McCoy
Lefty	Shorty
Manuel	Dutch
Cavalry Sergeant	2 Rustlers
Stolen Steer	

STAGE SET: the back of a chuck wagon at mid center; on each side of chuck wagon is a log or large block of wood

PROPS: skillet, spatula, 2 coffee cups, 2 plates, noose rope, a stick of catnip (ordinary licorice stick), a slice of pie, white broom bristle (cat whisker), patch of fur, tape measure

EFFECT: Sound — thundering horse hooves; cavalry bugle blowing "Charge!"

MUSIC: *Home on the Range*

COSTUMES: Cowboys all wear standard range drover clothes, with Vinegar Pete Flynn also wearing a white apron; Cavalry Sergeant wears a cavalry uniform; Rustlers have bandanas over their mouth and nose; Matilda wears a cat costume — ears, tail, whiskers, etc. in calico colors; Stolen Steer wears mask, horns, brown or black body-covering

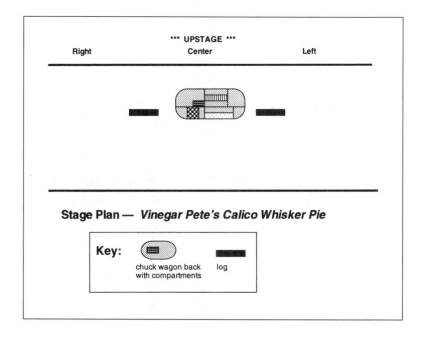

Stage Plan — *Vinegar Pete's Calico Whisker Pie*

*(LIGHTS UP FULL on the back of a chuck wagon at mid cen-
ter, flanked on each side by a log or large block of wood.
LEFTY and SHORTY sit on logs to right of wagon, sipping
from coffee cups; MANUEL and DUTCH sit on logs to the left,
with empty plates in their hands. HAYWIRE McCOY stands at
down right and addresses audience.)*

HAYWIRE McCOY:
> Haywire McCoy's what they call me;
> I've driven cattle for nigh thirty years.
> From Texas to the hills of Wyoming,
> I've followed the trail of the steer.
> I've seen dust storms and stampedes and earthquakes,
> Fought rustlers and renegades by the pile;
> Wrassled grizzlies as tall as an oak tree
> And rattlesnakes as long as a mile.
> But the strangest of sights I ever did see
> In my days 'neath the big Western sky
> Was the time our trail cook nearly got hung
> For serving Calico Whisker Pie.
> It was in the year of eighteen seventy-nine
> That I do this tale convene.
> We'd been on the drive for a month or so
> Headed for Sweet Abilene.

(Characters wave to audience as they are introduced.)

> Besides myself there was Lefty,

LEFTY:
> How do!

HAYWIRE McCOY:
> And Shorty from San Antone;

SHORTY:
> Pleasure!

HAYWIRE McCOY:
> Manuel was a bold vaquero,

MANUEL:
> ¡Buenas días!

HAYWIRE McCOY:
> Old Dutch a cowpoke from Cologne.

DUTCH:

Javol!

(BLACK JACK RAFFERTY enters from left; nods at other cowboys and stands somberly at down left, thumbs in his belt.)

HAYWIRE McCOY:

Our boss, it was Black Jack Rafferty;
He was stern but calm and fair.
Some said he'd been a gunslinger in Tombstone;
He exuded a most somber air.

(MATILDA, a calico cat, enters from right, stares for a moment at the audience and trots over on all fours to Black Jack Rafferty, who smiles and pets her head.)

LEFTY:

But the boss's expression would light up
In a smile as wide as the Platte,
Whenever he caught sight of Matilda—
His own pet calico cat.

SHORTY:

Now Matilda was more than a mouser,
Why, she was almost a regular saw!
She could ride drag as well as any cowboy,
And she loved her catnip chaw.

(Black Jack Rafferty Matilda gives Matilda a bite from a catnip stick.)

MATILDA: *(excitedly)*

Mrrrrrow!

(Matilda hops on a log and peers intently at the audience.)

MANUEL:

Perched on the boss's tall saddle,
She'd stand watch through the dark end of night;

(Lefty and Shorty shove each other; Matilda jumps down and crawls between their legs.)

MANUEL:

And if the boys ever got a little rowdy,
She'd be there to break up the fight.

(Lefty and Shorty laugh at Matilda's antics and shake hands; Matilda crosses to chuck wagon and begins pawing through the drawers.)

DUTCH:
You see, Matilda was the outfit's mascot,
Bringing good luck through thick and through thin.
And all of us range busters sure loved her—
All except Vinegar Pete Flynn.

(VINEGAR PETE, carrying a skillet, enters from right and trudges to the chuck wagon; a few feet short, he sees Matilda and yells at her.)

VINEGAR PETE:
Get away from my chuck wagon, you goldarn-picayune-gallnippin'-ramsquaddlin'-overgrown chunk of furry buzzard bait!

(Matilda glowers at him for five seconds, then hisses.)

MATILDA:
Hisssssssss!

(Vinegar Pete brandishes the skillet; Matilda daintily steps away from the wagon and goes to Black Jack Rafferty's side; Vinegar Pete goes to wagon and begins scraping skillet with spatula.)

HAYWIRE McCOY:
Now, Vinegar Pete was the camp cook,
The bean master and dough boxer, you bet.
A topnotch grub wrangler on the Old Chisholm Trail
For more than a decade, but yet—
Old Pete could be a moody cuss
As ornery as a coyote on the prowl.
And no cowpoke who favored his stomach
Would argue or cross him a-foul.

LEFTY:
One time when he cooked for an outfit,
Back in Nevada I recollect.
The boys thought the coffee tasted curious,
And the grounds began to inspect.

SHORTY:

> They found a vinegarroon in the coffeepot—
> That's a scorpion full of poison and bile!
> "Why, that cook's trying to kill us!" said one.
> "And he's not even cracking a smile!"

MANUEL:

> Old Pete he snarled and snorted
> And twirled his big butcher knife.

VINEGAR PETE:

> That vinegar juice has given you pep;
> It'll add ten years to your life!

DUTCH:

> So the boys they ceased to holler;
> They knew there was no use to wail.
> For sassing a trail cook is suicide—
> Like braiding a bronco's tail!

> *(Lefty, Shorty, Manuel and Dutch back away from Vinegar Pete.)*

HAYWIRE McCOY:

> Now the fellas on our drive kept their distance,
> Not wanting to spoil Pete's mood.
> Cause, by thunder, they wanted him happy,
> So they could keep eating their food!

> *(Matilda turns and stares directly at Vinegar Pete.)*

> But Matilda was the one creature among us
> Who didn't give Old Pete the air.
> In fact, she'd stare right at him,
> As if he weren't even there!
> And she loved to paw about in his chuckbox,
> Picking through odd drawers and bins.
> Following her feline curiosity
> In search of the sardine tins.

MATILDA: *(licks her lips)*

> Mrrrrrow!

VINEGAR PETE: *(puts down skillet and spatula, shakes his fists at Matilda)*

> Well, nubbins and jaybirds and taters!
> The next time I see that durn kitten,

I'll settle her hash full chisel, I will!
By Sam, I'll give her the mitten!
I'll sautée her whiskers and boil her ears,
I'll roll up her hind paws in biscuits!
I'll nip off her tail and whack off her ribs
Till she's saucered and blowed to a brisket!
Now, hear me out, one and all,
And don't you e'er forget it;
I'll have no more trespass upon my chuck,
Or such party will regret it!
If that darn cat dare stick her nose
Once more into my palace,
She'll be the sorriest four-legged beast
Ever lived from here to Dallas!

(Matilda glowers at him for five seconds, then hisses.)

MATILDA:
    Hissssssssss!
HAYWIRE McCOY:
    Well, the boys all figured Pete's tirade
    Was just his usual huffin';
BLACK JACK RAFFERTY:
    Come on, Matilda, pay no mind;
    That loco coot's just bluffin'!

(Matilda follows Black Jack Rafferty offstage left.)

LEFTY:
    But from that day forth when Vinegar Pete
    Had uttered his final decree,
    The drive took a desperate turn for the worse
    No one had thought to foresee.
SHORTY:
    We hit a stretch in the Staked Plains
    Where the sun ne'er ceased to gleam;
    We lost near fifty head to thirst
    Before we found a stream.
MANUEL:
    Then came a storm of rain and hail,
    That pounded down for days;

A score of calves were drowned to death
Right where they stood and grazed.
DUTCH:
Young Peppard from Missouri,
A lad we loved right well,
Died from a sudden snake bite
That caused his brain to swell.
HAYWIRE McCOY:
We lost two more to fever
And a fourth to lightning strike;
But the worst misfortune of them all
Was coming down the pike.
The boys began to talk in whispers
Furtive, low and grim,
About how the grub was ailing
And not worth diggin' in.
LEFTY: *(holds up coffee cup)*
This java tastes like turpentine;
It's as thin as wagon paint!
And the beans, why they're so powerful strong,
They'd make a buffalo faint!
SHORTY: *(points to Manuel's plate)*
The hash is like a river bottom,
All mushy and filled with sand;
The boggy top and bear sign
Are slobbery, beady and bland!
MANUEL:
I don't know what is the problem,
But, amigos, I am plenty concerned;
Ever since Matilda vamoosed from camp
Our lives — and stomachs— have turned!
HAYWIRE McCOY, LEFTY, SHORTY & DUTCH:
Matilda vamoosed! Holy calico!
DUTCH:
Sure enough, that cat's been gone a fortnight
Ever since the cook's uncouth outburst;
And have you noticed our luck has suddenly changed
From bum to bad to worst?

LEFTY:

    He's right, you know, there's something amiss;

    It's more than plain chance, I fear.

    Why, just last night those rustlers hit

    And stole another steer!

SHORTY:

    Matilda was our good luck charm;

    She always kept us in the pink.

    Why, if anything ever happened to her,

    Our lives wouldn't be worth tiddlywinks!

MANUEL:

    Oh, but who would harm such a beautiful cat?

    Who would trifle with our Fate?

DUTCH:

    Who, indeed, but a loathsome old worm

    Full of jealousy, venom and hate!

(Lefty, Shorty, Manuel, Dutch and McCoy turn and stare suspiciously at Vinegar Pete.)

VINEGAR PETE:

    Come and get it, you varmints!

    Stick your noses in the feed bag!

    Grab it now or I'll spit in the skillet!

    Wake up snakes and bite a biscuit!

(No one replies or moves.)

VINEGAR PETE:

    What in tarnation's wrong with you stiffs?

    Didn't you hear the banquet cry?

    Why, tonight I've made you all a special treat—

    Fresh-baked Calico Whisker Pie!

(Vinegar Pete holds out a slice of pie; Lefty, Shorty, Manuel, Dutch and McCoy recoil.)

HAYWIRE McCOY, LEFTY, SHORTY, MANUEL & DUTCH:

    Calico Whisker Pie! Gasp!

(Black Jack Rafferty enters from left and stands at down left, arms folded and staring intently at Vinegar Pete.)

HAYWIRE McCOY:
> Just then the boss strode upon the scene,
> The pure devil in his gaze;
> We all knew trouble was a-brewing sure,
> For Black Jack's temper was ablaze.

BLACK JACK RAFFERTY:
> A new dessert? Don't mind if I do!
> It sounds quite unique and refined.
> Why don't you let me be the first
> To sample what you've designed?

(Black Jack Rafferty crosses to mid center and is handed the pie plate by Vinegar Pete.)

VINEGAR PETE:
> Well, you're the boss and rightly so,
> You get to have lead crack;
> Eat your fill and stuff your gob;
> Need seconds? Come on back!
> But in all the years I've cooked and hashed
> Across the Western Plains,
> This is the finest cobbler sack
> I ever have attained!

(Vinegar Pete stands back, beaming proudly; Black Jack Rafferty inspects a forkful of pie, slowly raises it to his mouth, stops and puts it back on the plate without eating.)

BLACK JACK RAFFERTY:
> Before I indulge in this confection supreme,
> This specialty of your trade,
> Perhaps you would care to enlighten us
> As to the ingredients from which it is made?

(From out of the pie slice Black Jack Rafferty pulls out a long cat whisker and dangles it in the air.)

LEFTY, SHORTY, MANUEL & DUTCH:
> Matilda! Gasp!

HAYWIRE McCOY:
> With a flourish of his finger
> Faster than anyone could speak;

The boss upheld a whisker
From a delicate feline cheek!
He stuck his thumb into the pie,
Whence came a patch of fur;
And all the boys were stove-up sore,
Cause we knew it belonged to her!

BLACK JACK RAFFERTY: *(points finger at Vinegar Pete)*
By the great horn spoon, this is a deed
That for vengeance loudly hollers!
Boys, get a rope and let's commence
To stretch this cookie's collar!

(Manuel and Dutch grab Vinegar Pete and hold him in front of wagon; Lefty picks up a noose rope from the wagon and attaches it to wagon; Shorty takes a tape measure and measures Vinegar Pete's neck circumference; Black Jack Rafferty steps up to the wagon still holding the pie plate.)

VINEGAR PETE:
Now hold on, gents, just hold a sec,
There's been a terrible oversight;
That pie's not got a speck of meat—
It's a vegetarian delight!
Now the recipe is a family secret
Belonging to the ages;
I can't tell you everything it has,
But I'll impart the general stages.
First, I took some pinto beans—
Your basic border frijoles;
Then laid a bed of sorghum squash
And shaped 'em roly-poly.
A cup of prunes, a gill of salt,
Some mosquito knees and molasses,
A dose of skunk egg, a snip of grease
And a mix of prairie grasses.
Add to this some wild cherries,
An ounce of fried chopped suet,
A teense of tallow, cinnamon and crust—
That oughta just about do it!
But don't forget your splatter dabs,

Fluff-duffs and saddle blankets;
Two crossed eyes and a barbecued mist,
Plus a few raisins to gently spank it.
Throw in a dab of spotted pup
And a pinch of white goose syrup
Simmered in Texas butter and pork
Braised gently with a stirrup.
With a final smidgen of sugar and straw,
Some blackeyed peas and tartar,
Fried moonbeams and stewed snowflakes
And a dancehall angel's garter.
Since that's the makings of the pie in question,
There's no call for a necktie party;
The name? It's a sort of figure-of-speech—
I should have called it Alley Cart-e!

*(Lefty, Shorty, Manuel, Dutch and McCoy glower at Vinegar
Pete for five seconds, then hiss.)*

LEFTY, SHORTY, MANUEL, DUTCH & McCOY:
  Hissssssssss!
BLACK JACK RAFFERTY:
  Pete, you've spun a right fine yarn,
  But one fact you are forgetting;
  That cat of mine who's lately gone,
  Is in this pie, I'm betting!
VINEGAR PETE:
  Now, boss, you know that cat of yours
  Was awful inquisitious;
  Why, these bits of whiskers, fur and such
  She left poking in my dishes!
BLACK JACK RAFFERTY:
  Pete Flynn you are a cannibal,
  And a cold-blooded, stone-hearted fiend;
  I hereby sentence you to hang this day
  For puddinizing our Calico Queen!

*(Noose is thrown around Vinegar Pete's neck. SOUND —
thundering horse hooves and cavalry bugle blowing*

"Charge!." *A CAVALRY SERGEANT enters from left leading TWO RUSTLERS, their hands tied in front.)*

HAYWIRE McCOY:
Just as the noose was put in place
To work its gruesome task,
A sergeant of the cavalry arrived
With two hombres wearing masks.

CAVALRY SERGEANT:
These two brand blotters have full confessed
To raiding your herd for weeks.
They'll be jailed and tried in a court of law
And get more than a slap on the cheek.

HAYWIRE McCOY:
The boss began to give his thanks,
When the sergeant he demurred—

CAVALRY SERGEANT:
Don't throw your gratitude my way
It was *her* that saved the herd!

(Cavalry Sergeant points offstage left, and Matilda enters, riding a STOLEN STEER.)

LEFTY, SHORTY, MANUEL, DUTCH, RAFFERTY & VINEGAR PETE:
Matilda!

(Everyone gathers around Matilda at down center.)

HAYWIRE McCOY:
That kitten was ensconced aboard a steer,
Just purring to beat the band!
Turns out she'd disappeared from camp
To track that rustler caravan!
She'd stalked 'em through the desert
And trailed them day and night;
When she caught 'em they were so surprised
They couldn't even fight.

BLACK JACK RAFFERTY:
Matilda, you've plumb saved the day—

VINEGAR PETE:
Likewise my neck as well.

I'll never say an angry word
To my fluffy little mademoiselle. *(pets her head)*

(Matilda jerks her head away and glowers at Vinegar Pete for five seconds — everyone gasps! — then she meows sweetly and puts her head back under his hand.)

MATILDA: *(sweetly)*
Mrrrrrow!

(Everyone cheers.)

HAYWIRE McCOY:
So next time you're around the chuck box
And you get to feeling kind of sly,
Just ask if cook'll serve you a piece
Of Vinegar Pete's Calico Whisker Pie.

(Entire Cast sings "Home on the Range.")

ENTIRE CAST: *(SINGS)*
Oh, give me a home where the buffalo roam,
Where the cats and the antelope play.
Where never is heard a discouraging word,
And the catnip is blooming all day.
Home, home on the range!
Where the cats and the antelope play.
Where never is heard a discouraging word,
And the catnip is blooming all day.

(LIGHTS OUT.)

THE END

Home on the Range

**(words: Brewster Higley, music: Daniel Kelley,
arr. by L.E. McCullough)**

Oh, give me a home where the buf-fa-lo roam, where the
cats and the an-te-lope play. Where ne- ver is
heard a dis- cour- a- ging word, and the cat- nip is
bloom- ing all day. Home, home on the range!
Where the cats and the an- te- lope play. Where
ne- ver is heard a dis- cour- a- ging word, and the cat- nip is
bloom- ing all day.

Cavalry Call: "Charge!"
(traditional, arranged by L.E. McCullough)

A NOTE ON COSTUMES & SETS

If you are interested in creating really authentic costumes and material culture artifacts for your *Plays of the Wild West* productions, there are numerous books at your local library that tell how to do so. For individuals, you can consult biographies. Books on Annie Oakley and Buffalo Bill, for instance, offer detailed descriptions of what they wore along with photographs and portraits. Magazines such as *American Heritage*, *American History*, *Old West* and *True West* are also excellent sources for costume detail. Below are just a few books I discovered in the card catalogue at my local branch library:

- *Indian Clothing of the Great Lakes, 1740-1840*. Sheryl Hartman. Liberty, UT: Eagle's View Publishing. 391.0097

- *Traditional Dress: A Good Medicine Book*. Adolf Hungry Wolf. Summertown, TN: Book Publishing Co. 391.009701

- *Historic Dress of the Old West*. Ernest Lisle Reedstrom. New York, NY: Sterling Publishing. Also titled *Authentic Costume and Characters of the Wild West*. 391.0978

- *Calico Chronicle: Texas Women and Their Fashions, 1830-1910*. Betty J. Mills. Lubbock, TX: Texas Tech Press. 391.0976

- *Ceremonial Costumes of the Pueblo Indians*. Virginia More Roediger. Berkeley, CA: University of California Press. 391.09706

- *Mexican Indian Costumes*. Donald Bush Cordry. Austin, TX: University of Texas Press. 391.0972

- *Encyclopedia of American Indian Costumes*. Josephine Paterek. Denver, CO: ABC-CLIO. 391.09703

- *Cowboy Gear: A Photographic Portrayal of the Early Cowboys and Their Equipment*. Donald R. Stoecklein. Ketchum, ID: Dober Hill Press. 391.0978

- *100 Years of Western Wear*. Tyler Beard. Salt Lake City, UT: Gibbs-Smith Press. 391.0978

- *The Look of the Old West*. William Foster Harris. New York, NY: Viking Press. 917.8

- *Mexican Costume*. Carlos Merida. Chicago, IL: Pocahontas Press. 391.0972

- *$10 Horse, $40 Saddle: Cowboy Clothing, Arms, Tools and Horse Gear of the 1880s*. Don Rickey. Ft. Collins, CO: Old Army Press. 391.0978

- *Warbonnets*. Rod Peate. Denison, TX: Crazy Crow Trading Post. 391.09701

- **Anything** by author David Dary, whose comprehensive social histories of the American West include photographs, drawings and diagrams. Check out his *Seeking Pleasure in the Old West* (978), *The Buffalo Book* (559.7358), *Cowboy Culture* (978) and *Entrepreneurs of the Old West* (338.040978).

- *What People Wore: A Visual History of Dress from Ancient Times to 20th-Century America*. Douglas Gorsline. New York, NY: Dover Books. 391.09. This has a *huge* bibliography of other costume books.

THE AUTHOR

L.E. McCULLOUGH, PH.D. is a playwright, composer and ethnomusicologist whose studies in music and folklore have spanned cultures throughout the world. Formerly Assistant Director of the Indiana University School of Music at Indianapolis and a touring artist with Young Audiences, Inc., Dr. McCullough is the Administrative Director of the Humanities Theatre Group at Indiana University-Purdue University at Indianapolis. Winner of the 1995 Playwrights' Preview Productions Emerging Playwright Award for his stage play *Blues for Miss Buttercup*, he is the author of *The Complete Irish Tinwhistle Tutor*, *Favorite Irish Session Tunes* and *St. Patrick Was a Cajun*, three highly acclaimed music instruction books, and has performed on the soundtracks for the PBS specials *The West* and *Lewis and Clark*. Since 1991, Dr. McCullough has received 35 awards in 26 national literary competitions and has had 178 poem and short story publications in 90 North American literary journals. He is a member of The Dramatists Guild, Inc. and the American Conference for Irish Studies.